Medicine with a Human Touch:

Putting Patients First

Richard Dew, M.D.

Medicine with a Human Touch:

Putting Patients First

Richard Dew, M.D.

ISBN-13:

978-0615772127 (Dr. Richard Dew)

ISBN-10:

0615772129

To order additional copies of this book, contact Dr.

Richard Dew via

http://medicinewithahumantouch.com/contact.html

TABLE OF CONTENTS

CHAPTER ONE

The problem; Physician know thyself; The art of medicine; Caring and competence are both important; Attitude determines action; Medicine as a job; Medicine as a profession; Medicine as a calling; How you view patients determines how you treat them; Patients deserve respect; Without patients we're out of work; Treating patients is a privilege, not a right; Misguided humor isn't funny; Do unto others; Get to know your patients

CHAPTER TWO

First things first; Sit down and stay a while; There's a time to be serious; Err on the side of courtesy; The healing power of touch; Avoid all but the most urgent interruptions; Know who to talk to; Teenagers are people, too; Try to answer all of their questions; The unsolicited phone call; Forewarned is forearmed; Sometimes two heads are better than one; Talk in understandable language; Showing reinforces telling; You can't explain too much; Stay on schedule in the office; Stay on schedule in the hospital; Who's in charge?; Whose patient is it anyway?; Miscellaneous observations

CHAPTER THREE

Be methodical in taking a history; Encourage lists; Be considerate when taking a history; Use all the information available; Be considerate when doing a physical exam; Have a routine for doing a physical exam; If you code it as complete, be complete.

CHAPTER FOUR

We need to communicate; Make the consultant's job easier; What is expected from a consultant?; Criticism of others is never appropriate; Professional responsibility is always appropriate.

CHAPTER FIVE

Nurses want to learn more; Nurses can teach you, too; Be professional and responsive to Nurses; Make your orders legible and easy to understand; A concerned call requires concerned response; Criticizing nurses; A little praise goes a long way; Don't take yourself too seriously.

CHAPTER SIX

Know what you're talking about; Breaking the news; Honesty is the best policy; Who's in charge; Advise, don't dictate; Hope springs eternal; hospice can help.

CHAPTER SEVEN

Care doesn't end when patients die; They may be dead but they're still your patients; What do you do? What do you say?; Complete the death certificate ASAP; Care doesn't end with the death certificate; Know about the grief process ;Listening is often the best therapy; Grief is not usually clinical depression; Be familiar with other sources of help; Literature can be helpful; Writing can help; What not to say.

CHAPTER EIGHT

Help families remember; Reassure parents if you can; Support groups can be invaluable; What not to say after the death of a child; Parents grieve even if their child never lived; Support groups.

CHAPTER NINE

We can't afford to take care of ourselves; I'm so far in debt I'll never catch up; You need to know

business as well as medicine; How much do you
really need?; Many of us have a common malady;
a personal story; We need to see life differently

Be warned, if you take Medicine as a mistress, she will obsess you, but it will be a magnificent obsession.

ABOUT THE AUTHOR

I was eleven years old when I decided to be a doctor. Why the idea even occurred to me is a mystery. I had never been to a doctor, and the only one in the family was a distant great-uncle whom I did not meet until I was an adult. For whatever reason, while my friends were choosing to be firemen, pilots or cowboys, I opted to become a physician. When I was sixteen, I read *Not As a Stranger*, a popular novel about a young boy who followed a country doctor around and eventually became a family physician. It may seem strange that one's life journey could be so influenced by a potboiler novel, but somehow it struck a chord within me. From then on I was determined to emulate that book's protagonist. I had never been inside a hospital until my first day of medical school. Fortunately for me, medicine was all I had dreamed it to be.

After my internship, a tour in Vietnam as a medical officer, and my residency, I practiced family medicine for twenty-three years. At that time, for reasons I will explain later, I felt a need to change paths. A growing number of primary care physicians were opting to practice totally in their offices and were no longer seeing patients in the hospital. I had read about a new type of medical specialist called a hospitalist, who works entirely in the hospital caring for these office-based doctors' patients who need hospitalization. I started the first Hospitalist program in Tennessee and directed it for ten years. I now serve as the volunteer medical director in a community clinic for the uninsured.

As long as I am mentally and physically able, I doubt that I will ever quit medicine completely. I still get a rush from making a tricky diagnosis or stabilizing someone's diabetes. Even more fulfilling have been the relationships I've had with my patients, both recent and past. From them I have learned some of the poetry of life and the beauty and heroism of ordinary people, in their joy and in their sorrow, in their healing and in their pain. I remember talking once with the noted wildlife artist, Ray Harm. After knocking around for several years, he discovered his talent for painting. He said, "The person who can make a living doing what he loves to do is damn lucky." He was right.

INTRODUCTION

What is a good bedside manner? How do you tell patients they have a terminal illness? What do you do after you have told them? How do you deal with the family after a patient dies? How do you foster good relationships with patients, nurses and other physicians? How do you avoid burnout?

Your answers to these and similar questions will prove crucial to your medical career. Yet during my seven years of medical school and residency, these issues were never mentioned, much less dealt with. Some programs are now making efforts to teach the human side of medicine, but medical training today is not much different from mine. I intended *Medicine with a Human Touch* to be a guide for medical students and residents in dealing with these and similar non-medical problems. Yet numerous practicing physicians who reviewed it remarked that we would all do well to reexamine periodically how we are behaving in our everyday practice.

One of my major concerns in writing a book such as this is that I would come across as pompous, egotistical, and pedantic that my behavior always appeared exemplary, my diagnoses brilliant, and every treatment successful. Many of the negative things I mention, I have done. Most of the positive things I suggest, I did most of the time. Many of them, however, I learned through painful error.

The majority of the suggestions and pointers in

this book come from my own years as a family practitioner and hospitalist. Other insights originated from the critiques of students and house staff who have served preceptorships with me over the years. I am especially indebted to the medical and nursing staffs of Methodist Medical Center in Oak Ridge, Tennessee. I sought the views of physicians and nurses whom I knew were good dealing with patients. All had their own personal philosophies and practices, but the majority of the things I mention were on almost everyone's lists.

While they, and I, are far from perfect, we do practice many of the things presented much of the time. In so doing we have crafted a life in medicine that has proven rewarding and satisfying to us and to our patients.

I readily admit that my view of medicine and physicians is romantic. Physicians are special people, or at least we have the potential to be so. We certainly have the opportunity. We are allowed to enter where even priests are excluded. We must not take this trust lightly. Medicine can provide an array of moments of profound fulfillment, heartbreaking pathos, personal terror and uncertainty, and light-hearted levity found in no other profession. Unfortunately, for many physicians these moments glide by barely noticed, lost in what is to them the mundane drudgery of everyday practice. It need not be so. Each of us can learn to look at our life in medicine with different eyes and craft a career full of beauty and meaning.

My goal is to remind you of why you entered medicine in the first place and to instill in you my love of the profession. I hope this will point you toward a path of empathy, caring and concern that is often lacking in our modern, technologically oriented medicine.

I have tried to present what I know best -- practicing medicine with a human touch. While this book is not encyclopedic, it will give you a good starting point.

CHAPTER ONE
PATIENTS AND DOCTORS
THE PROBLEM

What happens then is like what happens when we separate a jigsaw puzzle into its five hundred pieces: The over-all picture disappears. This is the state of modern medicine: It has lost the sense of the unity of man. Such is the price it has paid for its scientific progress. It has sacrificed art to science.

-Paul Tournier, M.D.

I recently saw first-hand evidence of Dr. Tournier's concern at a major medical center in Memphis, Tennessee. My sister experienced some chest pain and made an appointment with her internist.

A nurse practitioner examined her and told her it might be her heart. A stress test was scheduled. A technician performed the stress test and informed the nurse practitioner that it was abnormal. The nurse practitioner told her she needed to have an arteriogram. The cardiologist's nurse called the next day and told her it had been scheduled.

By this time my sister was scared silly. She asked the nurse what an arteriogram was.

"Oh, the doctor just runs a plastic tube to your heart and injects some dye," she was told.

She then called me. I explained what would be done and the potential risks to her. Since she was frightened, I drove to Memphis to be with her during the procedure. At the hospital, she was admitted, prepped and pre-medicated. It was only after I insisted that the cardiologist came into the room and introduced herself. The arteriogram was done. A nurse told my sister it was normal.

She had multiple procedures costing thousands of dollars. If she had had an unusual complication, such as an intimal tear in a coronary artery, an angioplasty, stent or even bypass surgery would have been performed as an emergency. Yet, during all of this, she was never once examined by a doctor. In fact, no doctor ever spoke to her in an un-medicated state, and then only when coerced by me to do so. When I later examined the medical record, I found that from a brief hello and no examination the cardiologist was able to manufacture a three-page history and physical exam.

I spoke to several cardiologists about this and was told that "that's just how it's done."

Surely that is not the way it *should* be done. Was her experience typical of medical care   today? I don't think so but it is not unusual.

Not too long ago, physicians were far and away the most respected professionals. In a Gallup Poll taken in December, 2008, physicians ranked fourth, behind nurses, pharmacists and high school teachers. Why the drop in respect and admiration? There are many reasons, many of which we are powerless to alter.

With the emergence of HMOs and other managed care organizations, patients have less choice as to who their doctor might be. These choices may change each time an employer renegotiates the contract. When physicians are employed by these organizations, there is tremendous pressure to see as many patients as quickly as possible.

In addition, the public has unreasonable expectations from the medical community. Several times each week excited announcements of the impending cure for some horrible malady or eradication of a dreaded pestilence blare from our TVs and newspapers. I find it interesting to count how many times the qualifiers *may, could, might* and possibly are used in these breathless reports. They then disappear into some black hole seldom to be heard of again and are replaced in a day or two by the next miracle cure or silver bullet.

Patients now have almost unlimited access to medical information -- some   accurate,   some misleading, and some patently false − via the internet, television, and countless magazines. They can arrive in our offices as well-informed participants in their health care. They can also arrive as simply confused by, or frustratingly unaware of, the limitations of their newly found knowledge.

We can do little to change these things. But we are not without fault. In large measure we have ourselves to blame for our slipping regard and prestige. In many cases we have drifted away from being personable, caring physicians who are our patients' advocates in order to run more efficient practices and to be technically more proficient practitioners. Somewhere along the way we seem to have lost sight of the idea that the patient comes first. We have forgotten that the disease doesn't have the patient -- the patient has the disease.

PHYSICIAN KNOW THYSELF

*Oh would some power the gift might give us To see ourselves as others see us_*

- Robert Burns

"MD does not stand for Minor Deity." This small plaque has hung in my office since a patient gave it to me years ago. I think it was given in jest, but it serves as a useful reminder.

As with all humor, there is kernel of truth. Doctors have strong egos, which is good up to a certain point. The grind of medical school and residency require it. Physicians who are constantly second guessing themselves are seldom good physicians. There is, however, a fine line between self-confidence and perceived omnipotence. Doctors who don't know their limits -- who don't know what they don't know -- are a danger to their patients. Doctors who fail to stay current, who bristle when a colleague or a patient questions their diagnosis or treatment, or who take constructive criticism as a personal affront are just as great a danger.

Unfortunately, our ego problems often intrude into our relations with patients. Many physicians seem to feel that they are somehow superior to the great huddled masses who comprise the bulk of our patients. Listen the next time you're in a group of people who don't know you're a doctor. When the conversation turns to doctors, a primary complaint will likely be our perceived arrogant attitude.

More than once I've heard physicians, usually not too long out of training, upbraid patients for calling them "Doc." They tell patients in no uncertain terms that they studied eight years beyond college to earn the title, Doctor, and expect to be addressed as such. Their title with these patients, if the patients choose to remain, will forever be "Doctor Pompous Ass." It never dawns on them that, coming from patients, "Doc" is a term of endearment. I cannot recall being called "Doc" by anyone who did not genuinely care for me and hold me in high esteem.

We should remember that there are many other professionals -- teachers, nurses, and ministers to name a few -- who are just as dedicated and work just as hard as we do while receiving much less recognition and compensation. We need to keep it ever before us that respect must be earned -- it is not conferred with the title M.D.

THE ART OF MEDICINE

Throughout your career in medicine, you will sometimes come into contact with physicians who are held in unusually high regard -- yes, even loved -- by their patients. They seem too good to be true. What is it that sets this select few apart from their colleagues who are equally competent and often technically superior to them? I think it is primarily due to their uncommon grasp of the art, as opposed to the science, of medicine. The art of medicine is often referred to as "good bedside manner," but it is much more than that. It is the ability to recognize and appreciate each patient as a unique individual, to set them at ease, to listen with the heart as well as the head -- to really care.

For some, this capacity to empathize and to connect with their patients seems to be second nature, almost an innate ability. For others it is nearly impossible. But even those who are by nature aloof or introverted can certainly modify their behavior.

CARING AND COMPETENCE ARE BOTH
IMPORTANT

For many, it's not that they don't care. Their distance and detachment are often traits learned by observing brilliant but distant, detached mentors. They may simply have adopted such mechanisms to survive the crush of the mass of material that must be learned in such a short time. For whatever reason, many exit medical school and residency superbly trained in the knowledge and technology of modern medicine, but with little concept of how to relate to the very people upon whom their future career will depend.

A delicate balance exists between medical expertise and being likable. Perhaps the most dangerous physicians are those who are highly skilled but fail to know their limitations or recognize their own deficiencies. Equally dangerous are those who have wonderful rapport with patients but are clinically incompetent.

Make no mistake about it. Knowledge and clinical competence are the bedrock of good medicine. But, with knowledge and competence alone, you are little more than a highly skilled technician, and your patients will know it. To be a complete physician, you must also be nice. Most important of all, you must truly care. Your patients will know if you do.

ATTITUDE DETERMINES ACTION

The practice of medicine will be very much what you make of it: to one a worry, a care, a perpetual annoyance, to another a daily job, and to some a life of as much happiness and usefulness as can well fall the lot of man, a life of self-sacrifice, opportunities to comfort, to help the weak-hearted, and to raise up those who fall.

- Sir William Osler

Osler is correct. Your career in medicine will be pretty much what you make of it. Do you view medicine as a way to make a living, a track to upward social mobility, a pathway to public esteem, an intellectually stimulating profession, or an opportunity for service? Do you view patients as your adversaries, your clients, your source of income or your friends and partners in their health care?

I believe doctors approach medicine in three ways. Rather than three distinct, exclusive categories, these blend one with another and constitute a spectrum --- a bell-shaped curve with some physicians on either extreme, and the majority grouped in the middle. Once you have established your personal mode of practice, it is relatively easy to slip from the third level to the second or to the first --- to shift the curve from right to left − from good to bad to worst. It is difficult to progress in the opposite direction. The attitudes you develop in your training will most likely stick with you throughout your career in medicine and will determine to which group you belong.

MEDICINE AS A JOB

The first group regards medicine as a job, a means of earning a living. Many start out with noble intentions but later become disenchanted and finish their careers in this manner. They go to work, do what is necessary to pay the bills and fund the retirement plan, until finally, thank God, they can exit the rat race and retire. Though far from exemplary, we can understand them.

Less understandable are those who begin their practice in this mode. Perhaps they were first attracted to medicine by the lure of high income. Their emphasis is primarily economic. If it is good for business, do it. If it is the latest gimmick or fad diet plan, play it to the hilt. If there's money to be made hawking vitamins and dietary supplements from the office, go for it. Their office is usually the nicest in town, their equipment the most expensive, and their advertisements the flashiest. Many of the medical entrepreneurs touted in throw-away practice journals are in this group. Whatever will get the most patients through in the shortest period of time or will get the most income for the least effort is the goal.

Become this type of doctor and you'll probably make more money than most of your colleagues. But, you will be just what the managed care organizations and the government call you -- a vendor of medical care. Some sell widgets — you sell medical care. I know of no cure for those who practice this kind of medicine by choice. They don't want to be cured.

MEDICINE AS A PROFESSION

The second approach to medicine is that of a professional. Most doctors fall into this category, and it is light years better than merely looking upon medicine as a job. Professionalism has many aspects, such as our relations with other doctors, with nurses and with the general public. These will be addressed later. For now, I want to focus on practicing medicine as a professional. This group of doctors keeps up-to-date on the latest advances in medicine. They are meticulous in their practice, pay attention to details, and are conscientious in dealing with their patients. Hard work and reliability are their trademarks. If they are on hospital committees, they attend meetings and contribute. Their records are up-to-date. They make rounds predictably, and when on call they are available. They are intrigued by solving the puzzle of a patient's problem. In short, they are professionals. Professionalism is a necessity for all physicians, but often, as noted previously, professionalism is equated with being technically proficient. Too frequently, the patient is reduced to a disease, and a successful outcome is defined as discovering the proper diagnosis and treatment.

MEDICINE AS A CALLING

There is a third and better way, both for you as a physician and for your patients. That is the path suggested by Osler -- medicine as a calling or a ministry.

Although we're often too self-conscious or sophisticated to admit it, most of us first entered medicine because we genuinely wanted to help people. That desire still burns in us but is often dimmed by the pressures of too little time and an overfilled schedule. We can recover our first love if we work to become more aware of the enriching opportunities we overlook daily in our contacts with our patients.

Practicing medicine as a calling is professionalism carried one step further. Medicine becomes more meaningful as our patients become more meaningful. We are not providers of services as the government and managed care would have us be — we are serving professionals. We actively listen to our patients with an ear not only to their physical complaints but also to their spiritual and emotional pain and needs. No patient is too rich or poor, too bright or dull, too unfriendly or hostile to receive the best that we have to offer. We are patients' advocates in negotiating the thicket that is today's medical care establishment. We are their companions as they face the frightening specter of disease and its implications for their lives. Patients know when their physician really cares, and the benefits that come from this knowledge are great. Hippocrates said, "Some patients, conscious that their condition is perilous, recover their health simply through their contentment with the physician." He was right, and there is a growing body of knowledge to prove it. The benefits to us personally are manifold, but perhaps the most important is the opportunity to grow as we give ourselves to others.

HOW YOU VIEW PATIENTS DETERMINES HOW YOU TREAT THEM

It's three in the afternoon; you are three patients behind. There are eleven remaining to be seen, and you have just received a call that another has arrived in the emergency room. At this point most of us lose it. It's also at this point we make most of our mistakes in medical judgment and in our interpersonal relationships with patients. We become paranoid. They're out to get us. The patient has become our adversary.

If this occurrence were rare, it would have little impact on our outlook. Whether due to poor scheduling, poor time management, or too few physicians, situations such as these are becoming more often the rule rather than the exception.

C. S. Lewis maintains that the way we behave when stressed or caught unaware is a better indication of the type of person we really are than how we behave when we are rested, well fed and have on our church manners. In the same way, I believe the truest means for discovering what kind of physicians we are occurs when we are stressed, pressed for time or dealing with patients we find distasteful or unlikable. How we view patients is important because to a great degree it determines how we practice medicine.

Usually when we see patients, they are either ill or think they are. They are uneasy with our needles, tests, and specialized language, and often they are downright scared, sometimes with good reason. Just as we cut ourselves slack for our behavior when we are stressed or anxious, we owe patients that same latitude.

We must keep three basic facts about patients always in mind. We should write them down, frame them or put them on a plaque, but we should never forget them.

Fact#1

PATIENTS DESERVE RESPECT

Patients are the sole reason for our existence. They are the ones for whom we spend years learning to care.

Society recognizes their importance as citizens when it establishes standards of training before we can be licensed to treat them. Our government recognizes their importance through Medicare, Medicaid, and the myriad government-sponsored health programs.

Patients should be important to us as individuals. They are not interesting diagnostic puzzles to be solved. Neither are they merely broken nor flawed mechanisms to be mended or fixed. True, they do need to be diagnosed and treated. But they are living breathing people who deserve to be understood and respected.

Fact#2

WITHOUT PATIENTS WE ARE
OUT OF WORK

Patients are the ultimate source of our livelihood. This was much more apparent in the days before insurance, HMOs, and prepaid medical care. This is likely to re-emerge in the near future as more and more patients become in essence self-insured and begin to shop and compare fees -- and attitudes -- among doctors. We expect to receive good quality service at restaurants, in our schools, from entertainers, mechanics, builders and anyone else who charges us for their services. We cease to patronize those who demonstrate their lack of appreciation by indifferent or surly service. Patients feel the same about us. We are being paid well for our services. It is incumbent upon us to be sure that patients, at the very minimum, get their money's worth for the care we render.

Fact#3

TREATING PATIENTS IS A PRIVILEGE, NOT A RIGHT

A third thing that escapes many physicians is, that no matter how highly skilled we may be, patients are doing us a great favor by allowing us to treat them, not vice versa.

It is of paramount importance to remember this during our training. Medical students and residents are extremely bright and intelligent. However, in all honesty, if you, your wife or your child becomes seriously ill, are you going to have the top student in your class, or even the chief resident, care for them? I think not. We are their doctors because they are on the teaching service and have nowhere else to go. They are allowing us to learn medicine on them. In a sense, they are our guinea pigs. We owe them big time. When we are asked to see patients in consultation, they have little choice. They see whom their doctors tell them to see.

Similarly, with the rapid proliferation of hospitalist

programs, many of our patients don't choose us. They are either referred to us by their private physicians who do not admit to the hospital, or they are simply assigned to us from the emergency room. It is easy to forget that here, also, the patients are doing us a favor by allowing us to treat them. We are beholden primarily to them, the patients, not to the referring physician, the hospital or whatever group might employ us.

MISGUIDED HUMOR ISN'T FUNNY

"The Dork in Room 346 has a fever. He's the third Gomer from the left." These terms and many others are part of the vernacular of medical school and residencies. So are nervous quips after a strenuous but unsuccessful resuscitation attempt. We don't perform craniotomies, we crack squashes. I'm embarrassed to admit, but in my years of training I was quite adept at this lingo. We rationalized such language and behavior as an attempt to escape the stress that is a natural part of dealing with painful, unaccustomed events. But if this is so, why does it disappear from our vocabulary the moment we enter private practice? And why is it spoken almost entirely by males?

Obviously, there's a component of being macho and not showing signs of emotional weakness. I think there is also something else. As students and house staff we are immersed in learning about disease. Many times patients are incidental to this process. When we know little or nothing about them other than their illness, by and large, they are dehumanized. When we enter practice, we know our patients as individuals and identify much more closely with them.

When you're stressed by an emotion-laden situation, stop and think before you revert to this jargon. What if your spouse was the Dork? Or you heard laughter at the nurses' station immediately after an unsuccessful resuscitation attempt on your mother? It's not nearly so funny when it's personal.

BAD PATIENTS ARE PEOPLE TOO

We all tend to do well with "good" patients, but what are good patients? They are usually those who are near our own age, education, and social status, who possess a pleasant demeanor, and who pay promptly for our services. Unfortunately, there are not enough of these to go around. So how do we approach all patients as good patients?

Most patients are neither saints nor villains -- they are just people. While most are nice, or willing to be so, some have sour, negative dispositions. If we are honest, we must admit that some physicians have this same tendency. We need to take patients as they are, and we need to take them one at a time. Start viewing patients as a group and they become depersonalized and stereotyped, often characterized by the most bothersome one we have seen recently. In fact, each is an individual with a distinct set of beliefs, fears, anxieties, and prejudices.

As we see our patients, it is extremely important for us to know our own weaknesses and prejudices, and as best we can, keep them under control. I have great difficulty tolerating whiners. Give me a crotchety, plain-spoken stoic any day. A whining patient to me is like fingernails scraped across a chalkboard. Others relate poorly to old people, children, drug abusers, chronic pain patients, uneducated patients, patients on disability, uninsured patients, dirty patients, and hypochondriacs. We all have our hang-ups, but when one of these people shows up, hold your tongue, remain amiable and make an extra effort to understand or, at the very least, to tolerate them nicely.

It's almost always counterproductive to become short, angry, confrontational or a smart-aleck with a patient. When I have done so, almost without fail, it has come back to bite me. Tell them that they are not sick or it is all in their head, and they will become critically ill that night just to prove you wrong.

Even worse, they may unknowingly make you

confront yourself as I found out.

Mr. R. and his wife were immigrant Russian Jews who had been adopted by our local synagogue while they awaited permission to emigrate to Israel. Mrs. R. spoke little English. She was severely depressed and was brought to me by her sponsor, a patient of mine. Every week for three months, I saw Mrs. R. and, with the aid of her husband as an interpreter, I struggled to help her. These visits were always long, tedious and energy draining. If that were not enough, each time, after checking out, Mr. R. would ask to see me again for "just one more question." I hid my irritation as best I could and answered his questions. One day I had finally had enough. I was two patients behind and had been up most of the night in the emergency room. I was in no mood for the one more question that followed another trying visit with his wife.

"This time, he's just going to have to wait," I snapped at my nurse. "Let him cool his heels in the allergy room."

I left him sitting there for 45 minutes.

Mr. R. jumped to his feet as I entered the allergy room.

"What's the problem?" I asked, too sharply.

Seeming not to notice my attitude or his long wait, he grasped my hand in both of his and began speaking with his heavy Russian accent. "Dr. Dew, we will be leaving for Israel in three days. I want to thank you for being so kind and helpful to Nadia." He turned and retrieved a large coffee table volume of Rembrandt from the chair. It was obviously expensive, and he was obviously poor. "Please accept this as token of my appreciation."

I thanked him profusely, all the while searching for a convenient rock to crawl under.

Put your best foot forward, even when it's hard. Otherwise, it might end up in your mouth.

"DO UNTO OTHERS"

Always remember, patients are more than the sum of their symptoms. They are neither a receptacle for an illness nor an interesting riddle for you to solve. They are living, breathing individuals who deserve not only your skill, but also your respect. If you are not interested in each patient as a unique personality, you might be well advised to enter a specialty removed from close personal contact.

A wise general practitioner once told me to approach patients as if they were members of my own family and act accordingly, sort of a Golden Rule for physicians. As you interact with your patients, make it a habit to listen to yourself. If another physician addressed and treated you, your wife or child in the manner you hear yourself speaking to and treating your patient, how would you react? If another doctor spent the same amount of time with you or your family as you are spending with your patient, would you be satisfied? It even carries over into our case management. If you would insist that an MRI be done on you or your loved one but would not order one on your patient in similar circumstances because the HMO says no, you may rationalize it all you want, but you are an ethical fraud.

GET TO KNOW YOUR PATIENTS PERSONALLY

As best you can, get to know your patients. You can obtain superficial knowledge from their past and social history. You can't learn everything at once, but try to piece together a little bit more each time you see them. How do they handle pain and adversity? Be careful and don't over look a significant symptom because the patient is stoical. By the same token, don't over test and over prescribe because the patient is high strung and anxious.

How do they feel about doctors? In primary care, the vast majority of visits are from females. Perhaps because of their familiarity with PAP smears, mammograms and pregnancy, they are more amenable to preventative care. Males, for the most part, go to the doctor when they think there is a problem that needs fixing. Often there is. Just as strange noises in a car that has had no routine oil changes and tune-ups are more significant than in a well-maintained one, so it is with male patients. A visit by a male who has not seen you in three or four years is at the very least a red flag. Males are also often more difficult to convince that asymptomatic problems such as hypertension, elevated cholesterol, and early diabetes need to be treated.

What about their family? Anxiety and depression are more apt to be problems where there is marital discord, financial difficulties or troubled children.

By the same token, patients are pleased when you comment on their children's academic or athletic achievements. I keep a separate page for personal details, grandchildren, a trip to Alaska, a recent graduate, etc., and mention them from time to time.

Over time you become aware of their hopes, dreams and disappointments. This knowledge adds depth to your relationship with them and insight into their over all emotional and physical health.

Many of my most rewarding experiences have come from a seemingly insignificant interchange with a patient. The following is an example.

Jack, a janitor at a local manufacturing plant, was a nervous, twitchy fellow with a brusque, unfriendly manner. He was short, wiry, weighed only 128 pounds but had very labile blood pressure - not your typical hypertensive. I had struggled to control his pressure for several years with moderate success, but he remained flustered that "it wouldn't stay normal."

One day he came in seeming more on edge

than usual.

"What's the problem, Jack?" I asked.

"I've had this damned rash since 1942," he grunted as he tugged off the steel-toed work shoes revealing scaly, red feet with thick, cracked, fissured soles.

I did a scraping for fungal cultures. "That looks like a fungus. I saw a lot of it with the Marines in Vietnam but it usually wasn't this advanced."

"You were with the Marines?"

"Yes. I was, too. Where?"

Misty eyes gazed somewhere far beyond the walls of the examining room. His chin began to quiver, and in a hoarse voice he began to talk, as much to himself as to me.

"You know, I was going to be a doctor once. Accepted to college at the University of Alabama. Then the Japanese bombed Pearl Harbor. Joined the navy right after high school. They made me a corpsman and assigned me to the Marines. I was good, too. All the fellows said so. Called me 'Doc'."

He looked down at his feet. "Goddam rash started on Guadalcanal."

"How long were you in?"

"The whole thing. All the way to Okinawa." He paused. "Almost made it, too. But they overran us one night." His hands trembled and the distant gaze returned. "The next morning they dragged me and one other guy out from under twenty dead Japanese and Marines. Sent me home. Said I had combat fatigue. They were probably right. I never went back to college. I tried to once, but I just couldn't concentrate. I would've been a good doctor, too. Maybe it just wasn't meant to be."

I didn't know what to say, so I just sat.

"Oh, what the hell_ You think you can do something about this rash? And don't tell me to paint it purple with gentian violet. I did that fifty times. It doesn't work." For the first time in the years I had been seeing him, he laughed.

"There's some new stuff for funguses. I think we can help," I said.

"We're still in the medical profession, you know," Jack continued, "My daughter is a nurse at the hospital, and my son is an EMT in Atlanta. Not bad, huh?" "Not bad at all," I said. "Maybe they had a good role model."

A smile crept across his face. "Yeah, maybe they did."

Jack's rash cleared, and until he died three years later, he seemed a changed man. He was still anxious and twitchy, but his blood pressure was easier to control. When he came to see me he was more open and friendly. He wanted to talk about medicine and to tell me about his children.

A month after his death, his daughter came into my office.

"Something happened to Dad after he saw you

for his rash. He seemed more relaxed and, after forty-four years, he started to talk to us about the war. He wanted you to see these but wouldn't bring them in himself. He was afraid it would look like bragging."

She pulled a framed document and a small box from her tote bag and laid them on the examining table.

Beside the be-ribboned Silver Star, the document read, *For bravery above and beyond the call of duty.*

Get to know your patients personally. You might be surprised.

CHAPTER TWO

THE BASICS OF RELATING TO PATIENTS

This chapter deals with some of the nuts and bolts of relating to patients. While they may seem simplified and elementary, notice as you go about your business how many of these elementary items are ignored, even by experienced physicians. The thrust of this book is for medical students and residents. I was never taught any of these things. I picked them up by trial and, all too often, painful error. I hope this material will help you avoid some of these pitfalls. The suggestions are important and useful in the office as well as in the hospital setting.

Much of relating well to patients, and anyone else for that matter, comes down to common sense and simple courtesy. In our rushed routines we sometimes suspend both.

FIRST THINGS FIRST

First impressions are often lasting impressions, and you only get one chance.

When you first meet patients, introduce yourself and shake hands. As simple as this seems, doctors often neglect doing so, especially in emergency rooms and when rounding for another doctor. If family is present, introduce yourself to them also. Be sure they understand your name. If you have a card, it's helpful to give one to them. If your name is unusual or hard to pronounce, try to give them something light-hearted to remember it by. I usually tell new patients that my name is Dew, just as in Mountain Dew. Corny perhaps, but they seldom forget.

Make eye contact and smile. This should be automatic but is important when first meeting patients.

If you are uncertain how to pronounce their name, ask them and, if necessary, jot it down phonetically for future reference. It's hard to convince patients that you are personally interested in them if you can't even remember how to pronounce their names.

SIT DOWN AND STAY AWHILE

Once you have introduced yourself, sit down.

During discharge interviews with patient advocates at our hospital, patients almost always commented favorably if their physicians had done this. Most practice management consultants say it's inefficient and you should never sit when seeing a patient in the office. They are wrong_ Even if it is just a sore throat, sit down. In the hospital it is even more important. If there is no chair in the room, go to the nurses station and bring one back. This says to the patient,"You are important, and right now you are the sole focus of my attention. You can sit on the edge of the bed, but this is awkward and, in my case, I invariably disturbed the leg with the broken hip.

Studies have shown that you spend no more

time when you sit while talking to the patient than when you remain standing, looming over them. These same studies have shown that the patient perceives that you have stayed much longer than you actually have.

When you are running behind, try to avoid fidgeting and looking at your watch or giving other nonverbal signals that you are in a rush.

I have had patients tell me that certain physicians who saw them seemed so eager to get out of the room that a family member would stand in the door to prevent them from bolting until they had answered all of their questions. The memory of a hurried doctor will linger and will most likely be passed on to others, regardless of the outcome of the illness.

THERE'S A TIME TO BE SERIOUS

Don't make idle chit-chat the first time you meet patients or on visits with established patients who have new problems or concerns. Focus on them and their problem. Their primary concern is what is wrong with them and what are you going to do about it. How the local sports team is doing, what the weather's like, or even mentioning that you have the same home town is best held until the end of the visit or on a later one. Patients will be placed more at ease by your professional, but pleasant, demeanor and your obvious interest in them, than by the fact that you may have had the same third grade teacher. For the most part, especially early in the process, they are not interested in your history or personal problems, so keep them to yourself.

ERR ON THE SIDE OF COURTESY

Unless they are teenagers or younger, it is best not to address patients by their first names unless they have asked you to do so or unless you have asked and received permission. The fact that they may be a charity case, uneducated, unwashed, or just generally unsavory is no excuse to avoid showing respect by addressing them by their first names or, worse, taking no notice of their individual identities at all. Miss, Mr. and Mrs. are always appropriate. You are a professional and should conduct yourself as such. "Honey," "Dear," and other overly familiar terms are usually turnoffs for patients.

In a similar vein, most physicians are uncomfortable when patients address them by their first name. However much it may irritate you, this, as when they call you "Doc," usually indicates that the patient feels comfortable with you and is not a sign of disrespect. Correcting them seldom promotes good relationships or communication. It is best to grit your teeth, smile and move on.

THE HEALING POWER OF TOUCH

At some point during every visit with patients, physically touch them. Physical contact is especially important if the patient has AIDS or some other illness that they or the public view as loathsome. You normally touch patients during an examination, but try to do so even if you're just discussing test results and treatment options or giving counsel. Take their pulse, listen to their heart, or simply lay your hand on their shoulder. Bonding occurs with physical contact that happens in no other way.

AVOID ALL BUT THE MOST URGENT INTERRUPTIONS

While seeing patients, keep interruptions to a minimum. If you are expecting a call, inform them ahead of time. Don't take a cell phone in the examining room. In my office, I gave instructions not to disturb me except for calls from other physicians and nurses at the hospital. In the case of nurses' calls, I had my staff determine if it was an emergency or if I could call back in 5-10 minutes. If you are interrupted, always apologize and sit back down when you return.

KNOW WHO TO TALK TO

As soon as possible, get clear guidelines from patients or their caretakers who should be informed regarding findings and recommendations. Determine at the outset with whom you should or should not discuss their case. Remember, once you have lost a patient's trust, it is almost impossible to regain it. Even if patients say you may discuss their case with their family, it's a good idea to tell them and the family that you will do so, but only in their presence. Patients usually find it reassuring to know that you will not tell the family anything you have not told them first. It's also easier for you. Keeping track of what you've said to various parties is difficult. You will simplify things by being consistent and giving the same information to everyone.

Often a large number of family members are privy to the patient's progress. Let them know when you will be available and talk with them as a group. Try to appoint someone present to be responsible for informing anyone absent from the meeting. You will still be grabbed at the most inconvenient time by a late comer who just could not come when you talked with the rest of the family. Irritating as it may be, you will save time and ruffled feathers by smiling and telling them briefly what you told the others.

TEENAGERS ARE PEOPLE, TOO

Teenagers are people, too. As such, they have a right to your confidentiality even though this has the potential for problems.

For instance, in most states it is not necessary to inform parents when you prescribe contraception for teenagers. If they are sexually active, it's imprudent not to prescribe it. On the other hand, as a parent, I would like to know if my daughter were taking oral contraceptives.

I first talk with the teenage girl and discuss why she is sexually active. Often she says that guys expect it. I point out that if a guy does not think she's worth the price of a condom, why should she feel compelled to deal with the expense and risk of the pill just to please him. They usually nod, agree, and again request the pill. I strongly advise her at least to discuss it with her mother who will inevitably find out either by accident or by snooping. I then prescribe the pill.

Many times the teenager is brought in by a parent. Often parents will try to do all the talking and ignore their child. Try to talk directly to the teenager as much as possible. Sometimes the purpose of the visit is suspected drug use. If the teenager refuses a drug test, I do not order it even if the parent instructs me to. After getting whatever information parents want to give, I ask them to step out while I examine the patient. At this time, I get the teenager's view of the problem, make recommendations and ask what he or she wants me to relate to the parent. If they instruct me not to discuss anything with their parents, I don't. If the parent insists in being told what went on, I tell them to discuss this with the child. This approach sometimes works, but much of the time no one is happy.

TRY TO ANSWER ALL OF THEIR QUESTIONS

At the end of every office or hospital visit with patients, even for things as innocuous as colds, your last question should be, "Do you have any questions?" This ritual is one of the most important I ever developed. I encourage them to ask even if it seems silly and tell them I'd rather answer a silly question than have them leave with a silly worry. You may be surprised.

A good example was a teenager who appeared healthy but gave a very vague history and was obviously anxious. After trying to comfort her about what I thought was the problem, I asked if she had any questions. Almost in tears, she blurted out, "Can a hickey cause cancer?" I thought she would kiss me when I reassured her that not only would the red spot on her neck not turn into cancer and devour her but also that it would fade and disappear in several days. I doubt if it would ever have occurred to me to ask about that particular concern.

Every encounter you have with patients adds a little to their impression of you. Strive to leave the image of a competent, friendly, caring professional each and every time.

THE UNSOLICITED PHONE CALL

We all dread the stack of phone calls at the end of the day. Most of us have gone to great extremes to delegate as many of these as possible to someone else. I have found, however, that making an unasked for call can sometimes be a great time saver.

The most common situation is when I am caring for an elderly, disabled or demented person in the hospital or nursing home. I may miss the family when I make my rounds. If this happens two or three days in a row, I call the son or daughter. The contact number is always in the chart. Often they are at work. I apologize that I have not seen them and give them an update on their parent's condition. I then give them my plans for discharge. Doing so avoids the inevitable delay when they are unprepared for the discharge and impresses the family that I took the effort to call.

The hospital administration is impressed that the patient is discharged in a timely manner. I am impressed that I avoided the usual recriminations when the family doesn't see or hear from the doctor. An added bonus is that I get to talk at a time convenient for me, and that the call is kept short because they are at work.

Several situations keep me awake at night ---the febrile child with no obvious infection or the very ill adult with pneumonia who I think I can safely treat as an outpatient to name just two. I rest better if I plan to make a quick call the next day to check on how they are doing and arrange for them to return if necessary. Patients are always surprised and appreciative, but I am the main beneficiary.

UNCONSCIOUS IS NOT ALWAYS UNAWARE

Most seasoned physicians have observed episodes that defy explanation ---post-surgical patients who recall with amazing clarity events that happened while they were under anesthesia; the unconscious stroke patient who relates in great detail what the family said at her bedside; the agitated, but deeply comatose head injury patient who becomes quiet at the sound of his wife's voice.

I have seen these situations often enough that I do not say anything within comatose patients' hearing that I would not say if they were fully conscious. I take the family into the hallway for discussions I do not want patients to hear. I advise the family to do likewise. I explain that I don't know how much, if anything, of what we say is heard by patients. But I can only imagine how distressing it would be for me to hear plans for my funeral or disposal of my dearest possessions and be unable to participate in the discussion.

I also encourage families to talk to comatose

patients. I am not sure how much gets through. A familiar voice perhaps might be perceived and prove comforting. Wishful thinking? Superstitious mumbo jumbo? Maybe, but what is the harm?

Even if patients never hear a sound, it can be therapeutic for families to talk to them and can sometimes help families come to grips with their death. More than once I have had family members relate to me how healing it had been to tell their loved ones that they loved the more that they forgave some past wrong.

FOREWARNED IS FOREARMED

Beginning with your initial encounter, try to keep patients and their families current with what is happening and what is planned. When you have completed your history and physical, you should tell them what you think is wrong, what tests you will be running and what your treatment will be.

If the diagnosis is apparent ---pneumonia, for instance--- explain what pneumonia is. Tell them the usual length of hospitalization. Explain the typical course of pneumonia ---the fever usually lasts two to three days; the cough will linger longer; they will have a general lack of energy and stamina for a week or two. Give them an approximate time when they should be able to return to work. Some conditions such as broken hips and strokes usually require time in a rehabilitation facility. It is better to mention this early in the hospitalization so that patients and their families can become accustomed to the idea and make preparations.

Letting patients know what to expect allays much

unnecessary anxiety and avoids many unwanted phone calls.

SOMETIMES TWO HEADS ARE
BETTER THAN ONE

If you are uncertain, tell patients so. Don't try to bluff them. Patients appreciate honesty, coupled with your assurance that you are working hard to get them better and will do whatever it takes to help them.

If I am uncertain, or if patients seem uneasy with my approach to their case, I explain that I would like to consult another physician or seek a second opinion to see if some new ideas might arise. Sometimes they will decline, but they are set at ease that I don't want to miss anything and am willing to ask for help. Sometimes, a patient will ask for a second opinion even though you are convinced that what you are doing is correct. Taking this as a personal affront doesn't solve anything. Only two outcomes are possible. Either the second physician will agree with your management, in which case the patient's confidence in you is increased, or the second physician finds something you missed or had not thought of. In this case, the patient benefits, and you have learned something.

TALK IN UNDERSTANDABLE LANGUAGE

Most patients and families are unfamiliar with how doctors and hospitals operate. Explain what tests will be done, why you are running them and what you expect to learn from them. I have seen patients and their families in a panic because they were being taken for an unexpected echocardiogram, which they took to mean a cardiac catheterization. Two minutes of explanation beforehand would have avoided bruised feelings and a much longer conversation. When describing tests, test results and diagnoses, use common everyday language. Medical terminology is foreign to most people. This is demonstrated by the well-worn story about family members broadcasting far and wide that their father had suffered a massive myocardial fart and now had atrial tribulations. The doctor could have prevented misunderstanding and embarrassment by telling them their father had suffered a heart attack and had an irregular heart rhythm.

SHOWING REINFORCES TELLING

It's helpful to use models, pictures and diagrams to explain diagnoses and procedures. The next time a patient tells you that she has a hiatal hernia, ask her to tell you what a hiatal hernia is. Most haven't the foggiest idea. It's easy to draw a simple sketch, which will increase the patient's understanding. I carry a notepad in my coat pocket just for drawing rough diagrams of problems and procedures. In the office a small model skeleton and a book of medical illustrations help patients understand what you are talking about. If they understand what you're doing and why you're doing it, they're far more likely to follow your recommendations.

YOU CAN'T EXPLAIN TOO MUCH

Once you have diagnosed the patient's condition, explain the treatment in detail. This should include: how to take newly prescribed medicines and what side effects to look for, complications that could arise from the condition or treatment and what to do should they occur; Recommend life-style changes such as losing weight, exercising, and stopping smoking. It's a good idea to write a summary of this and give it to the patient for future reference. It takes a few minutes to write out an insulin sliding scale (less if you have it pre-printed) or to list all of the medications and directions, but if it prevents one phone, call you have come out ahead.

Ask patients to repeat what you have told them. Doing so will insure that they understand and can highlight areas where your explanations are less than ideal. Conclude all sessions with patients, but especially the one dealing with final instructions, by asking, "Do you have any questions?" Many would say that these discussions take too long, but in the long run they save time.

STAY ON SCHEDULE IN THE OFFICE

Patients hate to be kept waiting. Perhaps in no other area are doctors criticized as much as that of being late for appointments. For the most part, this criticism is justified. True, patients don't appreciate the very real problem of unplanned emergencies or dealing with people who schedule a brief appointment for a "cold" but in fact are there because they are depressed and contemplating suicide.

We doctors understand circumstances beyond our control. However, when our flight is delayed or when we make reservations at a restaurant a week in advance and find we still must wait over an hour for a table, we're not so understanding. Patients are no different from us.

I can't throw any stones in this area for I live in a glass house. I tried without success for 25 years to get my office schedule under control. Over time I made it better, but it was still far from perfect. Perhaps it can only be done by the growing move toward "boutique practices," where the doctor sees a limited number of patients who can afford to pay exorbitant prices for convenient care. But what about everyone else? What I have to offer may help you, and might mollify, but not completely satisfy, your patients.

The most common cause of being chronically behind is that we don't start on time. It is also the easiest to correct. When your first patient is scheduled to be seen at nine o'clock, see that person at nine o'clock, not after you have a cup of coffee, eat a donut with the drug representative and read the sports page. If you start out thirty minutes behind, I guarantee you will not catch up.

The second easiest thing to correct is not to over-schedule. Many significant mistakes are made because we're harried and rushed. If you have never seen more than six patients in an hour except during a flu epidemic, do not schedule 6-8 per hour.

Keep a record of when you most often get

behind and try to schedule a ten-minute gap at that time. I found that two such gaps each morning and afternoon worked best for me.

Some doctors use a "wave method" of scheduling appointments. A typical technique is to schedule four patients on the hour and three on the half-hour. Doing so insures you will have someone to see if a patient is late or does not show up for his appointment. But what if they all show up on time? Worse still, what if they are talking to each other and find that they are all scheduled for 10 a.m.? I never had the courage to try this scheduling method. I don't think I would be too happy if I found out my physician used it.

What do you do if, despite your best efforts, you are running 30-45 minutes behind? The first thing is to have your nurse or receptionist explain the problem to those waiting. Give patients an opportunity to reschedule. If they do reschedule, be sure they get an early morning or early afternoon appointment. They are not going to be pleased if they are rescheduled for the middle of another busy day when, in all likelihood, you will be as far behind as you were on the first visit.

The first thing you do when you are late seeing a patient is to sincerely apologize. This is the time to sit down and act as if you had all the time in the world, even if your ulcer is about to erode into your pancreas. I try not to lean too heavily on "medical emergencies" as an excuse. Before long, even the most obtuse patient realizes that nobody has that many emergencies. Saying something like, "Golly, everyone seems to have gotten sick at the same time today," eases my anxiety and often gets a smile although I am not sure how sincere it is.

If it becomes obvious that the visit is going to be much longer than expected, you can sometimes schedule another visit for the near future. This is simple enough when, in addition to their hypertension and diabetes, they want you to remove a wart. It is a little more difficult when the "cold" was in fact a severe clinical depression. Saying, "Hold that suicidal thought and see me next week," will not work.

I wish that I could be more helpful here. I never completely mastered the art of keeping on schedule in the office. Perhaps a management consultant could help. I tried this once without success.

In summary, make every effort to stay on schedule, recognize the patient's legitimate irritation when you don't, and offer a sincere apology when you are late.

STAY ON SCHEDULE IN THE HOSPITAL

Staying on schedule in the hospital is just as important as in the office. I had much more success here.

The most important thing is to start your rounds early enough to see everyone and get to the office on time. Nurses said they could set their watches by my rounds. If you have a large hospital census, start early. Assume the worst. I tried to start 30 minutes before I thought I needed to. If I finished early, I had time to complete some records. If I was running ahead of schedule, I called my receptionist and had her page me if an acutely ill patient walked in at the office or if my first scheduled appointment was early. The only thing better than starting on time is to start early, or to arrive early and have that donut and cup of coffee.

During my years as a hospitalist, I made rounds all day. The most important thing in this situation is to be flexible and available. I always saw the sickest patients first. Since I could not give families a definite time when I would be seeing their loved one, I had the nurse notify me when any family members arrived. Whenever I was called, I would break away as soon as possible and go see the family, even if I had been there earlier. Better to see them as much on their schedule as possible than to miss them and waste time smoothing ruffled feathers later.

WHO'S IN CHARGE?

"Nobody will tell me anything." In my ten years as a hospitalist, this complaint was all too common. It is understandable. When people are critically ill there may be five or six physicians involved to some degree in their care. Some doctors communicate better than others, but often even these are hesitant to discuss anything outside of their specialty. The pulmonologist will talk about the lungs, but not the heart. The cardiologist will discuss the heart, but not the lungs. The surgeon who removed the gall bladder will not venture an opinion on either.

When multiple doctors are involved in one patient's care, it is important that someone be the primary spokesperson. Even when they are all responsive to the patient and family, and are saying essentially the same thing from the perspective of their specialty, the patient and the family perceive that each doctor has said something different from the others. Someone needs to correct misunderstandings or tie up the loose ends into one comprehensible whole. If you are the patient's regular physician, the responsibility is yours. In many cases patients are referred to the hospitalist either directly from their primary care physicians or the emergency room. In such a case, the hospitalist is the obvious person to communicate. When there is more than one hospitalist, try very hard to have the same doctor see the patient daily.

It is difficult enough for physicians to keep everything straight in complex cases. Look at it from the view point of patients and their families. In a time of extreme emotional stress, they are trying to make sense of what is going on, and they don't even speak the language. We need to help as much as we can.

WHOSE PATIENT IS IT ANYWAY?

With the rise of multi-doctor groups, the concept of "my patient" seems to be fading. We have multiple rationalizations for our lack of response, but often it's simply a matter of inconvenience. This problem rears up primarily in the emergency room, especially between 5 p.m. and 9 a.m. One of emergency room physicians' most common complaints is that they can't get doctors to come in to admit their own patients. Patients are infuriated by long hours spent in the emergency department awaiting admission. While there are multiple reasons for delay, a major contributor is that hours may be spent trying to coerce a doctor into admitting a patient who often is their regular patient. Many patients still do not understand why their physician does not see them in the emergency room. They understand it even less when their physician is reluctant to come to admit them. I always took the approach that if patients thought I was their doctor, I was their doctor until I had made other arrangements. If I was on call for one of my partners, I was the patient's doctor until the next morning when my partner would assume their care.

MISCELLANEOUS OBSERVATIONS

The two greatest stimuli for patients to pay at the time of service are a tactful, gracious secretary and a friendly, caring doctor. I doubt many patients are ever moved to pay by a sign at the checkout window instructing them to do so. For many patients, this sign reinforces the view that doctors are money driven. Besides, what are you going to do if they don't pay?

Many malpractice suits arise when patients believe their feelings are ignored, or when they are angered by a real or perceived lack of concern and caring. The best malpractice insurance is a physician who really cares about his patient and transmits this to them.

When a patient brings you a gift, it is out of sincere affection for you. Keep a box of stationery in your office and send a thank-you note that day or the next. Also jot a note in the chart and mention the gift on the next visit.

CHAPTER THREE

THE HISTORY AND PHYSICAL EXAMINATION

Time and again we have heard, "Patients will tell you what is wrong if you will just give them a chance." Perhaps this is repeated so often because it is true. With the advent of sophisticated diagnostic tools, the art of taking a thorough, in-depth history is being pushed further into the background. The availability of technology combined with the pressure to see more patients in a shorter time, has resulted in situations where snap judgments and tunnel vision based on first impressions of the initial complaint are all too common.

We are urged to hold down medical costs. Many CT scans, MRIs and abdominal series could be avoided by a thoughtful history. I will frequently see a patient who has been to the Emergency Department with headaches and has had two CT scans of his head within six weeks of each other. I doubt the ER physician thought they had developed a brain tumor in this short period. The doctor just didn't take time to find out what had previously been done.

Spending an extra ten or fifteen minutes on a more comprehensive history and physical will produce huge dividends in accuracy of diagnosis, avoidance of unnecessary tests and time and medical resources saved.

A personal experience will illustrate this point. I was called to the emergency room to consult on a patient who presented with a sudden onset of paraplegia. A neurologist and the emergency room physician had been working for over six hours and had run the entire gamut of tests related to paralysis but had made no diagnosis. I asked the patient to tell me when he first noticed anything different and then bring me up to the present. He said he developed a stomach ache and back pain two days before. The pain lasted several hours and eased off. When he woke on the day of admission he could not move his legs and was brought to the emergency room. With this in mind, I laid my hand on his abdomen and felt a huge pulsatile mass. Just as his history suggested, he had ruptured an abdominal aortic aneurysm that then had tamponaded, preventing a fatal hemorrhage. The interruption of blood flow had infracted his spinal cord. This was not brilliance on my part but the result of taking time to listen to the patient rather than stampeding for the laboratory. Awakening with paraplegia leads down one diagnostic path. Abdominal pain followed by back ache, followed by paraplegia leads points to an altogether different, and correct, pathway. With this history, any good senior medical student should have made the diagnosis. Without it he would have been floundering.

BE METHODICAL IN TAKING A HISTORY

You should develop a consistent routine for taking a history and doing a physical.

A good way to begin the history is to ask patients when they first began to feel as if something was wrong and have them bring you chronologically up to the present. Let them talk. Several studies have shown that doctors interrupt patients on an average of every fifteen to twenty seconds. Just sit tight and listen. When patients have finished, you can then ask questions to fill in the gaps. If they begin to ramble, gently redirect them.

It's also a good idea to do your history and physical before reviewing any tests and X-rays that were done by the emergency room physicians prior to their calling you to see the patient. This helps you avoid tunnel vision. Your history and physical should guide the tests you order, not vice versa.

I won't elaborate each element of the medical history, but you skip over any of them at your peril. One case illustrates this well.

I was called to the emergency room to admit a patient with a severe, persistent cough. He could barely talk due to his coughing. In the weeks prior to this trip to the ER he'd had two chest X-rays, skin tests, a bronchoscopy and a CT scan of his chest. All were normal. In reviewing his medications, I noted that he was taking an ACE inhibitor. He had started this one week before the onset of his cough. With no further testing, I discontinued this medication, and his cough was gone in two days. Every medical resident knows that the most common reaction to an ACE inhibitor is a cough, but up to this point no one had noticed what medication this patient was taking. As in much of medicine, the devil's in the details, but often so is the diagnosis.

ENCOURAGE LISTS

As you take your history, act interested and show concern for the patients' problems. It may be old hat to you, but they are anxious, at best, and may be scared out of their wits. Because patients are nervous, they forget. I ask them to bring me all their medications and to make a list of things they think are important. In the hospital I encourage patients and their families to keep a notepad by the bedside and jot down what they want to ask. If they don't, invariably they will think of two things that are important to them right after I leave the room. Most of us were told early in our training that when patients come in with a list, they are most likely "crocks." Much time and valuable information are lost because we accept this erroneous assumption.

BE CONSIDERATE WHEN TAKING A HISTORY

When taking a history in the hospital, try to provide the patient with as much privacy as possible. If there is a conference room or an examining room on the floor and the patient's condition allows, go there. Often there is no such place or a patient is unable to be moved. Politely ask any visitors in the room to leave. If there is another patient in the room, ask their visitors to excuse you for a few minutes also. Shut the door and pull the curtains.

If a patient is forgetful, confused or demented, ask a family member or someone who seems to be in charge to remain and help you with the history. A light-hearted statement to the patient such as, "I'm going to ask your daughter some questions about your health. If she says something that you disagree with, feel free to correct her." This often sets everyone more at ease, especially if once or twice while taking the history you address the patient, smile and ask, "Now, is she telling it right?"

When a third party must be used to assist in taking the history, the patient and the family appreciates it if you address your questions to the patient whenever possible. Ask the patient even when the daughter is giving the answers. Try to avoid appearing to ignore a patient or referring to her in third person. In a similar vein, include the patient's spouse in obtaining the history, even if the spouse is elderly and the children can answer with more speed and accuracy. Being old is bad enough. Being ignored is worse.

USE ALL THE INFORMATION AVAILABLE

A final but important part of the history is to review any old records that are available. It's embarrassing, not to mention a waste of medical resources, to tell a patient that the CT scan you ordered was normal, only to have them inform you the one done two weeks ago in the emergency room of another hospital was also. While much helpful information can be obtained from old records, don't rely on the previous physician's history and physical for information you should gather yourself. The history of medicines and allergies is notoriously inaccurate.

When you have finished your history, it is helpful to ask if the patient has any questions or wants to add any information.

Always keep in mind that far more diagnoses are missed and more errors made from taking an inadequate history than from ordering too few tests.

CLEANLINESS IS NEXT TO GODLINESS

Most of us exit medical school well-trained in the skills of doing a thorough physical exam, and there is no need to reiterate what we were all taught. This section deals with complaints I have heard repeatedly from patients. We give rise to these complaints because we are rushed, or fatigued or have slipped into bad habits.

The first seems so mundane that it should not require

mentioning. Each and every time you examine a patient, wash your hands. It seems so basic, but watch others. Watch yourself.

Hand washing is important to prevent the development and spread of resistant bacteria. Nurses are very conscientious about this. Doctors are often less so.

In the office, washing my hands when I first enter the room assures them that I have done so. I learned this by painful experience. One day soon after I had entered practice I started to examine a woman. "I didn't hear you wash your hands after you left the patient in the next room. Did you?" she asked. Caught and embarrassed, I had to admit I had not. I forgot very seldom after that. This may seem nitpicking on the part of the patient, but it is an important nit to pick.

BE CONSIDERATE WHEN DOING A PHYSICAL EXAMINATION

Patients appreciate it if you warm your hands and stethoscope before examining them. Females appreciate it if you provide them with a sheet or a blanket to wrap in while they are waiting in their paper negligee. They appreciate it even more if you will also warm the speculum before doing a pelvic exam.

If at all possible, have patients sit fully clothed in a chair while waiting for you and while you take their history. It may be more efficient for them to be disrobed when you enter the room, but do not do this. In our training, every physician should be required to give a medical history while perched on an examining table trying to hold the edges of a flimsy paper gown together. This would be even more realistic if we had sat in an air-conditioned room to the point of near hypothermia before our examiner even entered.

Help the patient on and off the examining table, especially if they are elderly, obese, arthritic or pregnant.

Let patients know what you are going to do before doing it. Gently touch the perineum with your finger before inserting the speculum into the vagina. When doing a rectal exam, touch the anus for an instant to warn them that you're ready and to allow a bit of relaxation before ramming your finger home. When you are done, extract it slowly to spare them the sensation that they have just crapped on your floor.

HAVE A ROUTINE FOR YOUR PHYSICAL EXAMINATIONS

When doing an examination, have a routine and methodically stick to it. This applies not only to a full physical exam but also to your more limited exams on hospital rounds. For patients with pneumonia, you should obviously listen to their chest daily; this applies also to other patients who are bedfast: post-op patients, those who are debilitated or those who have had strokes or broken hips. Detecting rales in their lungs before they develop full-blown pneumonia will decrease morbidity, mortality and length of stay.

Check their calves daily. A DVT is much easier to treat than a pulmonary embolus.

There is one situation where I have found it useful to depart from my usual order of conducting a physical exam. I examine the problem area last. If a patient comes in because she found a lump in her right breast, I examine the left one first. She may have a cyst in the right breast, but an undetected cancer in the left. If a patient complains of lower abdominal pain, I check the upper abdomen first. It's important to diagnose diverticulitis, but it is also important to find an enlarged liver or spleen.

Take advantage of any opportunity you may have to examine patients, especially those who seldom see a doctor. As I noted before, this is particularly important in the case of reluctant male patients. They may have come in for an ingrown toenail, but if their blood pressure is elevated, notice it and treat it. During a flu epidemic, I made it a point to do breast exams on all of the women ---they were stripped to the waist anyway ---and prostate exams on all of the men who would allow it. They all had the flu, but two had prostate cancer and one had breast cancer.

When older patients see you for a respiratory infection, it only takes an extra few seconds to listen for carotid bruits. If you're checking their abdomen, listen for bruits and palpate to see if the aorta is dilated. An ounce of prevention really is worth a pound of cure.

IF YOU CODE IT AS COMPLETE, BE COMPLETE

A complete physical exam is just that ---complete. Remember the old saying, "Where do you hide a fifty dollar bill from a cardiologist? In the rectum or vagina." You should never "defer" a rectal or breast exam unless the patient instructs you not to do one. It is embarrassing, not to mention legally risky, to cure a pneumonia and miss a cancer of the rectum or breast. It is doubly so when you did not do the exam but dictated it as normal. If you did not do it, do not say you did.

CHAPTER FOUR

DEALING WITH DOCTORS

Just as patients come in all shapes, sizes and temperaments, so do doctors. Some are a joy to work with; some are a pain in the butt. Just as we must take our patients as they are and do our best to get along with them, so it is with our colleagues. We may not even like certain physicians, but we should always try to be cordial and professional in our dealings with them.

WE NEED TO COMMUNICATE

"Dr. Dew, Dr. X wants you to consult on the patient in 405," the nurse informs me.

"What is it about?"

"He didn't say and nothing is written on the chart. He did say it was urgent."

When I arrive on the fourth floor, the nurse hands me the chart. Sure enough, there it is. *Consult Dr. Dew ASAP.* There is neither history nor admission note to be found. I page Dr. X, but the operator tells me that he is gone for the day. I reach his partner who is on call tonight. He's apologetic but knows nothing about the patient. What to do next? Go ask the patient, who in all likelihood has no idea who I am or why I have been summoned? Check with surgery to see if the patient has been scheduled for an operation?

Farfetched? No such luck. Similar things happen daily in every hospital across the country. Usually the result is just lost time and personal irritation. But, many of the catastrophes that occur in medical care have their origin in the simple failure of physicians to communicate with each other. Why don't we pass the information vital to the care of the patient to the other doctors involved? The most common reason given is lack of time. We forget that five minutes of conversation, or at a minimum a legibly written note, can prevent hours spent in the ICU explaining misunderstandings to families or weeks spent trying to justify our action to a jury in the courtroom.

Communication is an overused buzzword. Webster defines it as transmitting or imparting knowledge; giving or interchanging thoughts and information. Entire careers are dedicated to teaching "communication skills." The communication between physicians that I am talking about is not complicated. In fact, it is very simple. I don't want to delve into Dr. X's psyche. I just want to know why he consulted me.

The advent of electronic medical records may be a golden opportunity for improving doctor to doctor communication if for no other reason than preventing the need for deciphering our handwriting. The note, however, still must be legibly written or typed up. The following suggestions are things that I have tried to do throughout my career. They are apropos for a two-physician office or a thousand bed medical center.

MAKE THE CONSULTANT'S JOB EASIER

Whenever you consult other physicians, make a personal call to tell them why you want them to see the patient. If you are seeking advice about an outpatient, send a note describing the purpose of the consult. Be sure to FAX pertinent office notes, lab and X-ray reports. If consultants' office staffs often misplace this information, have patients hand-carry these notes to their office.

In the hospital, talk with the consultant personally and be sure the history and physical has been transcribed and is on the chart. If this is not possible, at least have a detailed, legible note explaining your findings and what you seek from the consultant.

Always explain to patients and the families whom you are consulting and why. If they prefer Dr. X, and you feel he is equally skilled as Dr. Y, get Dr. X.

Many times they will ask whom you would recommend. Here, the rule mentioned earlier holds. If you would prefer Dr. Z to see you or your family member, the patient also deserves Dr. Z.

When you request a radiological study, give the reason on the X-ray request form. Many times, despite your best efforts, this information does not get to the radiologist. If the X-ray report does not reflect what you were concerned about, call the radiologist. On cases that are more than routine, I try to go to the X-ray department and view the films with the radiologist.

One of my pet peeves is being consulted to see a patient whom the attending physician has not seen. My hair still bristles recalling the many times I was called by the nurse in the middle of the night to see a post-op patient with a fever just because the surgeon did not want to get out of bed.

I cannot remember a single case, day or night, when I called for a consultation without first evaluating the patient myself and then personally calling the consultant. I felt I had no right to haul someone out of bed if I was unwilling to get up myself.

WHAT IS EXPECTED FROM A CONSULTANT?

When the roles are reversed and you are the consultant, especially if there are several specialists on the staff in your field, there are several things that will prove vital to your success. Remember, most patients don't know any specialists from whom to choose and will rely on the recommendation of their doctor. So how do you become the doctor to whom other physicians want to refer?

First, and foremost, you must have skills equal to the other specialists. If you do not stay current and get consistently good results, no conscientious physician will use you except for the simplest of problems.

Referrals will be few if patients complain that the consultant did not treat them with respect and consideration.

When you hospitalize patients who were referred to you, let the referring physicians know when they were admitted and where they are. Be sure referring physicians get timely information about their patients' hospital stays. Keep referring physicians informed of your findings and recommendations. You should also do this in consulting on outpatients. This is best done by a personal call, which gives the referring doctors a chance to ask questions. It also offers you an opportunity to tactfully teach them if their diagnostic tests or treatments could be improved. If you tell patients to follow-up with their private physician in two weeks, be sure this information is there in two weeks. Patients think that we spend hours discussing their particular case with each other. There is nothing more embarrassing than to see patients and know nothing about what was done and what medications were prescribed. Don't make the referring physician appear stupid.

During my years as a hospitalist, I designed a one-page form which listed the diagnoses I made, the medications I prescribed, pertinent lab and X-ray results and any suggestions I had for follow-up. I filled this out by hand at the time of discharge and faxed it to the primary care physician at the same time I wrote my discharge orders. In this manner, everything attending physicians needed to know was in their office before the patient left the hospital. It was also a handy outline for dictating the discharge summary right then.

This may vary from doctor to doctor, but I looked to my consultants to help educate me and keep me current. I tell them point-blank that if I miss something or if I make an error; I want to know about it. If there is a new medication or diagnostic test that I ought to be using, I want them to tell me about it. I appreciate it when they do ---and so will the patient.

CRITICISM OF OTHERS IS NEVER APPROPRIATE

Physicians do not like criticism of their care or treatment. If a perceived shortcoming is not significant enough to tell the physician in person, it is not important enough to blab to the other doctors, the nursing staff and most certainly not to the patient.

I have never understood why a physician would criticize another physician to a third party, other than perhaps for the transient sense of feeling smarter or superior. What's the point?

Never criticize a nurse or another physician in the medical record. Airing your grievances publicly will make you appear petulant and immature to any nurse or doctor who may read the chart. More importantly, this type of note is a malpractice attorney's best dream.

If a significant diagnosis was missed or improperly treated, correct it and inform the patient what you think the diagnosis is and how you are going to treat it. If the patient asks me why Dr. X did not do as I'm doing, I usually respond that I don't know. Perhaps the circumstances were different when he made his diagnosis. (Perhaps they were.)

If there was a significant mistake, I inform the other doctor what I found, what I did and what I told the patient. If it was an egregious error, there are appropriate means in all hospital medical staff bylaws to insure that it won't happen again. However, we must have the gumption to use them.

PROFESSIONAL RESPONSIBILITY IS ALWAYS APPROPRIATE

What about the physician with drug or alcohol problems? Or the one who exceeds his skills and training? Our patients rely on us to police our own ranks. Too often, we look the other way, hoping nothing serious happens. I'm embarrassed to admit that I have done this on occasion. When medicine is as important to you as it is to most of us, it is agonizing to think that you might be curtailing or ending a colleague's career. I hope I did the right thing on most occasions.

A local surgeon had not seemed his usual self and twice had needed help to bail him out of cases he had previously handled with ease. One morning I saw him heading toward surgery, literally bouncing from one wall to another. I called the Surgery Chief and the Chief of Staff. He was not allowed to enter surgery, and his privileges were suspended pending investigation. Tragically, he was in the early stages of pre-senile dementia and was self-medicating. In two years he had full-blown dementia. He never practiced again.

Physicians have a high incidence of substance abuse. We have all known doctors who have drinking problems. Usually we learn of this through the hospital grapevine. Nurses talk about receiving slurred or nonsensical orders in the middle of the night. We smell alcohol on their breath. What should we do?

If the doctor is your friend you could talk with him/her. If you are hesitant to do so, write a formal report to the Chief of Service or Chief of Staff. If no action is taken, every state licensing board has a mechanism for rehabilitating impaired physicians. Use it. I had to do so only once. I felt bad, but I had no regrets.

CHAPTER FIVE

NURSES

As noted earlier, nurses are ranked by the public as the most admired professionals. This reputation is well deserved. Many times physicians overlook the significant contributions they make to quality patient care.

My major shortcoming was my dealings with nurses. For the first 20 years of my career my relationships with nurses were rocky. In fact, much of the time I was an overly critical jerk. Most of the problems that I present came not from observing other physicians, but from looking in a mirror. Many of the more astute observations came from interviews with nurses.

NURSES WANT TO LEARN MORE

We must always remember that nurses are fellow professionals. Many have spent almost as much time in training as physicians have. For patients to receive the best possible care, doctors and nurses need to function as an interconnected, cooperative team. We all give lip service to this idea, frequently more in the abstract than in actual practice.

Most nurses are eager to learn but are sometimes hesitant to ask questions. Take a minute to point out what you are doing with a patient and why. Explain why you chose a certain mode of therapy or one drug over another. Doing so can help prevent misunderstandings when patients later ask the nurses questions about aspects of their care.

If a patient has an unusual reaction to a medication, such as a cough from an ACE inhibitor, point it out to the nurse. When you hear a heart murmur or a friction rub or find a swollen calf, demonstrate it to the nurses and explain their significance. Do this in the patient's presence. Their understanding of their condition and their perception of the quality of their care increases when they see their physician in this teaching mode. An additional benefit is that if you do this often enough, you will notice that over time the nurses begin pointing these things out to you.

NURSES CAN TEACH US, TOO

Ask nurses for their opinion about patients' physical and mental status. They are with them far more than we are. Pay attention to nurses' observations. Many an overconfident resident has come to regret ignoring the experienced nurse in the newborn nursery who says, "That baby just doesn't look good." In my experience, such a comment called for heightened vigilance and observation.

If you decline a nurse's request for a change in the patient's care, rather than barking out a gruff, "No," explain your reasoning in a friendly manner. A typical example would be limiting opiates in a patient with severe COPD who has significant CO_2 retention or restricting them from a patient you know to be a drug abuser.

Seek the nurses' views on patients' family situations and dynamics. Far better to deal with Aunt Sally's minor, or sometimes major, peeve before it becomes an item for confrontation.

I made it a practice to scan the nurses' notes in the chart. If a geriatric patient is becoming confused at night, it's easier to explain sun-downing to family members immediately rather than later being blind sided in the hallway when they are frantically asking about mother's "stroke".

Many times there's humor buried in nurses' notes. I

remember with some consternation the run-on sentences that read *Dr. Dew at bedside. Passed large liquid stool.*

BE PROFESSIONAL AND RESPONSIVE TO NURSES' CALLS

Be courteous and positive when responding to nurses' calls. Contrary to what we may believe, nurses almost always try to limit calls to those they feel are necessary. Negative, sarcastic remarks on our part are never appropriate. If we step back and examine the situation objectively, usually we will agree that the call was needed. Our sarcasm and negativity are usually prompted by a previous pattern of such behavior, being tired, or more commonly, being inconvenienced. Being brusque and nasty when nurses call seldom diminishes the number of calls. If it does, as I found out more than once, it could be to the patient's detriment.

MAKE YOUR ORDERS LEGIBLE AND EASY TO UNDERSTAND

As you make rounds, notice how many times two or three nurses and often a unit secretary are huddled trying to decipher an illegible or confusing doctor's order. Sometimes they will try to enlist your aid in doing so. Sometimes it will be your order. We're responsible for our orders being legible and easy to understand. We should not be upset if we are called when they are not. I assumed that if an order could be misconstrued, it would be. It's much easier to explain a complicated order when we write it than to clarify it in the middle of a busy office schedule.

A CONCERNED CALL REQUIRES A CONCERNED RESPONSE

Never leave nurses hanging. If they call about a problem, deal with the problem. "What do you expect me to do," is never an acceptable response, no matter how tired or irritated we are. Many medical disasters happen when on-call physicians convince themselves that the nurse is overreacting. They then try to apply some temporary patch to the problem until morning. I found that, rather than grilling the nurse in an attempt to find an easy way out, the best thing to do was to ask in a friendly voice, "Would you like me to come see the patient?" If the answer was yes, I went. It took me twenty years to learn to do this.

CRITICIZING NURSES

Nurses make mistakes, just as doctors do. When we

make a mistake, how do we want it dealt with? Nurses don't appreciate public humiliation anymore than we do. Pitching a fit at the nurses' station accomplishes nothing. Hurling an instrument across the operating room is more a demonstration of the surgeon's pettiness and immaturity than of the nurse's perceived incompetence.

Before we criticize a nurse, we need to be sure that criticism is warranted and the level of response is appropriate. Medication errors will be made and will need to be corrected. Every hospital has a mechanism for doing so. The goal is to prevent further mistakes, not to cause public embarrassment.

As with doctors, don't criticize a nurse in the presence of others or in the medical record. If the problem is minor, discuss with the nurse, in a nonjudgmental manner how it happened and how it can be prevented in the future. If it is more serious, discuss it with the nursing supervisor or the Director of Nursing.

All hospitals have their version of an incident report. It should be a tool for risk management and not a means of getting back at a nurse. One way we can foster this idea is by filling out an incident report on ourselves when we make a mistake or when our illegible or ambiguous order results in an error.

A LITTLE PRAISE GOES A LONG WAY

Nurses make mistakes, but, more often than not, what they do is praiseworthy. When nurses are especially compassionate with patients, let them know that you notice it. Mention to patients what a good job their nurses are doing. If they make good diagnostic pick-up, compliment them, preferably in the patient's presence. If they do something exceptional, compliment them to their supervisor or, better yet, write a complimentary note to the Director of Nursing.

DON'T TAKE YOURSELF TOO SERIOUSLY

If you have been curt or rude with a nurse, sincerely apologize at your first opportunity.

Doctors are human. Nurses realize this, even when we don't. It helps when they see that we really understand our own humanity also. This fact was driven home to me several years ago. I use this true story when I am giving talks or workshops for nurses. They all seem to enjoy it. I wonder why.

I was called to the ER to admit an elderly gentleman who was having rather brisk rectal bleeding. He strenuously objected to admission because he had a large inguinal hernia and, in his excitement over the bleeding, he had left his truss at home. After much persuading, he relented and entered the hospital.

When he was ready for discharge, I gave him instructions and a prescription for iron pills. As is so often the case, a few minutes later the nurse sought me out and told me that he had one more question.

I found him standing stark naked by his bed. A huge hernia bulged from his groin. In his hand he held a 4x12 inch cloth pad to which was attached several belts and buckles.

"They gave me this truss to wear," he said. "Can I keep it?"

"I didn't even know we had anything like that," I replied. "If you've used it, I'm sure no one else wants it. It's yours."

"I can't get it on. Could you help me?"

Trapped, I gave in. I reduced his hernia and pressed the pad over it. "Hold this while I get these belts adjusted," I instructed him.

As I struggled with the apparatus, unbeknownst to me, the nurse entered the room. She stood to the side and let me dig myself in deeper and deeper. Finally, with an amused smile, she stepped in.

"Dr. Dew," she said dryly, "I believe that's his wrist restraint."

I'm convinced that she told this story to the entire nursing staff within 48 hours. It has now become a permanent part of our hospital lore.

The most frustrating thing for me was that if she had just given me five more minutes, I would have made it work.

CHAPTER SIX

END OF LIFE CARE

He was one of the best surgeons I ever knew. His judgment was superb and his operative skills were unsurpassed. Residents competed to be on his service. As far as I could tell, he had but one flaw in his armor. If he was unable to cure a patient, he took it as a personal failure. Postoperatively, as soon as such a patient was stable, he ceded most of the care to the residents. I'm sure this was unconscious on his part, but if you observed closely, more often than not, as we approached the room of a patient whose cancer had been beyond resection, he would disappear. The cause for his hiatus on rounds was perfectly logical from his perspective: he had an important phone call, he needed to check an X-ray or pathology report or discuss something with the head nurse. The interruption lasted until we were ready to move on to the next patient. Perhaps his action was for the best. I'm sure patients sensed his problem. Some even apologized for failing to respond to his therapeutic efforts.

While this surgeon's behavior was extreme, it is to some degree imbedded in all of us. We became physicians to cure illnesses, not watch them ravage our patients despite doing our very best. That all our patients will die if we don't die first is of little consolation. Of necessity, we must adapt to the reality that many of our patients will die despite everything we do.

Dealing with terminally ill patients is difficult, but it need not be approached as an onerous burden. I have received some of the most profound insights into the human condition from patients who, knowing that their time is limited, have shed the superficialities that cloak many of our daily lives. I have been inspired by the calm courage and, often, eager anticipation with which they approach the next phase of their existence.

The care of patients with illnesses that have a high probability of death requires accuracy, honesty and compassion: accuracy in diagnosis and treatment options, honesty in discussing prognosis and the benefits and risks of treatment, and compassion in dispensing this information.

Cancer is one of the most common examples of an illness requiring end of life care of any duration. Advanced cardiomyopathy, end-stage pulmonary disease, AIDS, hepatic and renal failure and progressive neurological conditions such as ALS fall into the same category and require a similar approach. I will use the model of a metastatic malignancy, but the underlying principles of care are for the most part interchangeable.

KNOW WHAT YOU'RE TALKING ABOUT

"You have cancer until someone proves you don't." My thoroughly frightened patient quoted the ER physician in a city where she had been on business and developed rectal bleeding. Her bleeding proved to be a hemorrhoid that was cured with a rubber band. Perhaps the ER doctor was just trying to make sure that she would follow up when she got home. I'm convinced he could have dealt with her in a less melodramatic fashion.

Early in the diagnostic evaluation establish who, if anyone, the patient wants present for all discussions. Everyone can then ask questions and clarify their understanding of what is said. Much like the old game of gossip, telling the same thing to three people separately often results in three different perceptions of what is to be done or what has been determined.

To many patients the word "cancer" has death knell connotations. We should not be haphazard in its use. During my residency, an internist told me, "It's not cancer until the pathologist says it is." Remembering his advice has helped me to avoid needlessly alarming patients. CT scans, MRIs and other advanced diagnostic tools allow us to predict diagnoses with more certainty than in times past, but they are not infallible. I remember two middle-aged patients with weight loss, enlarged lymph nodes, funny lymphocytes, and abnormal liver function tests. They appeared to have some form of lymphoma. I was relieved I had heeded my mentor and did not mention lymphoma when they both proved to have an unusual adult presentation of infectious mononucleosus. We have all seen the ominous looking chest X-ray that, rather than cancer, proved to be loculated fluid, an odd fungal infection, sarcoid or some other benign or treatable condition.

Patients will often pressure you for a diagnosis before the work-up is complete. As soon as the words "abnormal chest X-ray" or "elevated blood count" are mentioned, patients automatically assume that they have cancer. I have found it helpful to give them a brief list of the possible diagnoses such as infection, inflammation or scarring from some previous condition, while not omitting cancer. If they press further, I tell them that I can't know until our tests are complete and the pathologist has it on a slide and tells me what it is.

Some would view such hedging as being dishonest if I really think it is a cancer. However, I want to avoid giving erroneous information. It allays the patient's apprehension to some degree but admits the possibility that it could indeed be cancer.

BREAKING THE NEWS

Once a cancer is diagnosed comes the hard part --- breaking the news. How we inform them has a lasting impact on the patient and the family, even when the cancer has a good probability of a cure.

A friend of mine gave me a verbatim description of her Friday afternoon post-mammogram visit.

"You have cancer of the breast," her physician blurted without preamble. She described herself as being stunned and, mouth agape, staring at him. Obviously ill at ease he continued, "I guess I've spoiled your weekend, haven't I?"

She has never been to him again.

What we say and how we say it have profound effects and merit serious preparation. This is not a time to "wing it." After we have been in this situation many times, we become more adept at handling it, but even the most experienced doctors would do well to pause and rehearse what they want to say and accomplish.

If the patient wants family members or others to be present, be sure they are there.

Try to have an environment that is conducive to delivering bad news. Turn off your pager and cell phone. If you are dealing with an outpatient, hold the discussion in your office with comfortable chairs rather than in the treatment room with the patient teetering on the examining table and the family propped against the walls. In the hospital having the discussion in the room is fine, if it is a private room. Be sure there are places for you and everyone present to sit. Turn off the TV. If there is another patient in the room who cannot be removed for a few minutes, try to find somewhere with some privacy, even if you must go to another floor. Many hospitals have no area suitable for quiet, serious meetings with patients. There may be a small staff conference room nearby that will suffice. I have commandeered the nurses' lounge when nothing else was available.

Decide ahead of time the primary information you want to convey and what decisions should be made during this visit. Use language patients and their families understand. Avoid medical jargon. Make eye contact and speak directly to the patient. Deliver a small amount of information at a time. Pause periodically to be sure they understand what you've said. I will say something like, "I've dropped a lot on you, and I understand this is rough. You may not be thinking too clearly right now, but do you have any questions?"

However you handle it, when you've finished, always ask if there are any questions and give those present time to formulate them. I tell patients that they may think of several questions after I have left. I advise them to keep a note pad by the bedside on which they and family members should jot down any questions that they think of later (or that they and their friends gather from the Internet). Don't forget to get their list and answer as best you can on your next visit.

HONESTY IS THE BEST POLICY

Once you've reached the point of discussing treatment options and prognosis you should have some idea of how patients and their families receive and process information. Unless they are mentally or intellectually unable to understand what you are saying, I think it is always best to deal directly with patients. Family members may be present if patients want them. Get an idea about how much information they want. One way of finding out is to say the following or something similar: "Some people want a lot of details, while others prefer just a broad overview of the big picture. Which do you prefer?"

Whatever information you dispense and however you relay it, you must always be empathetic, but honest. Families will often request, "Don't tell mother that she has cancer. She couldn't handle it." I attempt to avoid this slippery slope. I try to explain to them that most often mother already has a good idea that something is seriously wrong. Unless she is a total dunce, she will certainly guess when we start talking about possible surgery or chemotherapy. Once she discovers that I have been dishonest with her, I can never regain her trust in me as a physician or an advisor.

The final point I try to impress on them is that it is not fair to force mother, at the end of her life, to play games. To pretend that everything is okay and to coerce her into playing along is cruel. Tough decisions must be made that deal with her and her physical and emotional well-being. She should have the ultimate input into these decisions.

When considering a dire illness, focus on delivering the prognosis without giving false hope. With any serious illness, potentially fatal or otherwise, a good approach is to help the patient to hope for the best and plan for the worst.

Such an approach allows you to discuss the worst possible outcome without eliminating the possibility of long term remission or cure. The same approach applies to discussing treatment options. What would be the result of a best case response to treatment? What would be the next step if a particular treatment fails or if there are serious complications from the therapy?

Being open and honest is often hard for a physician. But in the long run taking any other course is even harder.

WHO'S IN CHARGE?

In many cases of a terminal illness, several physicians care for the patient. All too often the old adage "when everyone is in charge, no one is in charge," is true. In the case of an advanced cancer, the oncologist usually is the main caregiver.

All physicians involved in the patient's care should share information about what they've recommended or said to the patient to avoid sending mixed messages to the patient and family. I find it helpful to also pass the same information to the nurses caring for the patient. Note all dealings with the patient in the chart and, if need be, transmit them personally to the other physicians, especially discussions of prognosis and treatment options.

Primary care physicians should be a vital part in the care team even if they never write an order. Their primary role is to aid in coordinating the efforts of all physicians and to ensure continuity of care. They should take the lead in explaining in understandable language the need for, and the purpose of, tests and treatments that the patient is undergoing.

Patients often rely on their primary care physicians to give unbiased opinions and advice and to provide perspective to the ongoing course of the disease. These physicians should also offer emotional support through the ups and downs of the illness. Empathetic listening is often one of the most helpful treatments a dying patient receives. It is often one of the least administered.

ADVISE, DON'T DICTATE

The 95 year-old mother of a friend of mine developed significant rectal bleeding. She had a Living Will and had designated her daughter to make her medical decisions. She was alert and cognizant. The gastroenterologist scheduled her for a colonoscopy. The lady had informed her daughter and her physicians that under no circumstances was any surgery to be done. With this in mind the daughter told the physician to cancel the test. Nevertheless, her mother was kept on clear liquids. That evening, the nurse brought in the half-gallon jug of bowel prep. The daughter sent it back. In short order the young doctor came and urged her to allow the procedure. When the daughter remained adamant, the doctor said, "I bet I could talk her into it."

"You do that, and I will file suit the next day," was the mildest portion of the daughter's reply.

He made no further efforts.

The mother is now 97 and doing well.

The point is that patients have veto power over all tests and treatments. They are always reassured when we tell them this at the outset of our discussions with them. If we feel they are making a poor decision, we should explain firmly, why we feel they should decide otherwise. If they choose to disregard our advice, then we do the best for them that we can. Ultimately the decision is theirs.

Some physicians dismiss from their practice patients who do not follow their recommendations. They do so even in situations that are not imminently life threatening such as the severely emphysematous patient who won't quit smoking or the alcoholic who won't quit drinking. (Refer back to discussion of good patients and bad patients.) I don't fire patients for noncompliance. I tell them that I will do the best I can with whatever limitations they want to impose, but they should not expect a good outcome.

HOPE SPRINGS ETERNAL

"Hope" is the thing with feathers

That perches in the soul

And sings the tune without the words

And never stops at all.

                                        - Emily Dickinson

    Hope is a vital element in the treatment of a terminal illness. We need to nourish and engender hope as we care for these patients, not destroy it. At the same time we must always be honest and not promote false hope. We also need to realize that hope is a moving target.

The initial hope is always that the illness will be cured. Many times it's apparent from the outset that such hope is not realistic. Some patients, however, may not be ready to accept that a cure is not possible. I don't recall ever telling a patient, "There's nothing we can do." They interpret this to mean, "My doctor doesn't want to treat me anymore." There is always something you can do.

Sometimes the only thing to do is to protect them from spending their last days in a frantic search for a cure. Some people feel that they must exhaust every option. In such a situation, I try to convince them that they should go to one major cancer center and follow the recommendations made there rather than jump from one institution to another.

We should try to protect them from things that could be harmful. I try to dissuade people from choosing quack cures when there are therapies with proven benefit for their condition.

As options become fewer, it is helpful on every visit to ask, "Do you have any questions?" If they seem uneasy talking about it, it's often helpful to preface questions with something like, "I understand that this is difficult to discuss."

If they ask a question, answer it as honestly as you can. If possible give positive as well as negative information, for example: 25% of people at this stage live two years while 75% die within this period.

As their condition worsens, hope narrows: I hope you can control my pain. In almost all cases, we can. There's one caveat, however. Many physicians do not use enough pain medication for fear of legal complications or of promoting addiction. With careful titration most patients are reasonably comfortable and alert on dosages that ordinarily would induce coma or death. I know of no one who has been prosecuted for fraudulent drug prescribing in the care of a terminally ill patient. As for the fear of addiction, the patient is dying, for Pete's sake.

They are especially sensitive to our actions or inactions that they perceive as negative such as not coming to see them or seeming rushed or distracted when we do come. This is a time to sit down, listen, answer questions and give them our undivided attention.

HOSPICE CAN HELP

If the patient is willing, I have found it invaluable to get hospice involved. Hospice workers are most helpful if they are contacted early ---the last 3-6 months of a patient's life. There is not much they can do if the patient is nearly moribund when they are first called. Hospice nurses and workers are experts in dealing with the myriad physical and psychological problems associated with a terminal illness, and they have the time to be in the patient's home frequently. The only downside is that when we ask hospice to help in their care, patients often feel that we are abandoning them. Sometimes they are right. Reassure your patients that you will still be in charge of their care. Continue to see them on a regular schedule. If they become bedfast and unable to come to the office, make a house call. The inconvenience of a home visit will be offset by the appreciation of patients and their families.

CHAPTER SEVEN
WHEN PATIENTS DIE

In the eyes of many patients and families, we physicians don't handle death very well. Though some doctors may view having a patient die as a failure, I think the main reason we struggle is that we just don't know what to do or say. There were 125 doctors on the staff of our hospital, all of whom I had known for years. Yet, outside of my partners, only six of them ever personally acknowledged the death of my son. I hope the following material will help us do better.

CARE DOESN'T END WHEN PATIENTS DIE

"Dr. Dew, I've wanted to tell you this for a long time. My family will never forget what you did the day mother died."

This unusual office visit beginning stopped me short. I remembered her mother well. Martha had been a funny, vivacious old lady - a delight to know and treat. She reminded me very much of my own mother. Other than her puckish sense of humor, the thing that stuck most in my mind was a ritual that began at the end of her first visit.

"Sonny," she said, as I helped her down from the examining table, "I like you."

She then proceeded to plant a sloppy kiss on my cheek.

"Well," she said, as I stood there red-face, "aren't you going to return it."

Somewhat clumsily, I pecked her cheek. And so it went, every visit, for the next seventeen years. She died at age 92 of a massive stroke. I remembered her, but, at that moment, I hadn't the foggiest idea what I did the day she died. That had been four years ago.

"Sarah, I remember Martha, but I can't recall what I did that day," I confessed.

Sarah choked up a moment, then continued, "When you came and pronounced her dead, you kissed her on the cheek, just like always."

Then I remembered. I didn't know anyone had seen, but as I leaned over her body listening for the heart that had quit beating, it seemed the natural thing to do. I don't make a habit of kissing corpses, and I doubt that I ever did it to another patient.

From this little incident I learned that families are remarkably sensitive to what we say or do when their loved one dies.

They are especially sensitive to our actions or inactions that they perceive as negative such as not coming to see them or seeming rushed or distracted when we do come. This is a time to sit down, listen, answer questions and give them our undivided attention

THEY MAY BE DEAD BUT THEY'RE STILL YOUR PATIENTS

What we do, or don't do, when a patient dies has effects far beyond the legal pronouncement and release of the body to the funeral home. Although no two situations are exactly alike, there are some practical steps that you can take that will help both you and your patients' families through a very tough time. Our dealings with bereaved families fall into two main categories: the immediate aftermath of a death and the long-term support we need to provide later.

In the past people were not dead until a physician said they were. Nurses can now officially pronounce patients dead. What difference does it make who pronounces them? None to the person who died. But it can mean a great deal to the family. Unless it is impossible, I always pronounce patients personally. If they have been long- term patients, I owe them one last show of respect.

If patients are in the hospital or a nursing home, I ask the nurse if the family is present or if they are coming. If they are there, I go then. If they are coming to the facility, I ask the nurse to call me when they arrive. Not only does the family appreciate the physicians presence, but also the nurse who is not saddled with trying to answer clinical questions the family may have or, even worse, trying to explain why the doctor is not coming. If the family does not come, I tell the nurse to fill out the forms and release the body to the funeral home.

If patients die at home, I try even harder to go. The family is often alone with no support. Many times the police must be notified if the physician does not go. If the police are not involved, the only alternative the funeral director has is to haul the body to the Emergency Room of the nearest hospital where someone will pronounce them dead. If your mother or father died at home, is this how you would want it handled?

In addition to showing your care and concern, you can also answer any lingering questions the family may have about a loved one's condition or treatment.

.

WHAT DO YOU DO? WHAT DO YOU SAY?

What do you do when a patient dies? What do you say? What follows is a distillation of what I have learned from forty years of family practice and from my experiences in dealing with over a thousand bereaved parents. Some situations, like the death of a child, are particularly difficult. I will discuss these in the next chapter.

There are some things that help in most circumstances when we are caring for grieving families.

The most important thing is to be there. There is nothing you can do in absentia.

What do you say? The best thing is "I am so sorry." Nothing we say can fix the situation. Anything we say beyond a simple expression of sorrow has the real potential to do more harm than good. Platitudes and clichés, pious or otherwise, seldom help and often infuriate the family. The bereaved may use those terms, but we should not.

There is nothing wrong with letting our emotions show. If we get choked up, or even shed a tear, no harm is done (unless it is to the extent that the family winds up comforting us). They may not notice. If they do, they will remember it favorably. We need to bear in mind that the self-control that we prize so highly is not of paramount importance - but compassion is.

I have told medical students, "Don't just do something, stand there." An example of this adage's application occurred several years ago. The elderly mother of seven had an intracerebral hemorrhage but was stable. As was the custom in our area, all the immediate family, and some not so immediate, were crowded in the hospital room. Her condition worsened, and I sent her for a CT to ascertain if she had extended her hemorrhage. While in X-ray, she died. When I told the family there was instant pandemonium. People were screaming, fainting and pounding the walls all around me. The nurse dashed in and asked if she should get a syringe of Valium. I told her no. "Well, what do you want me to do?" she shouted, almost as agitated as the family.

"Why don't you just close the door?" I suggested and stepped to the side of the room.

In about fifteen minutes things slowly quieted. The oldest daughter, who seemed to be the leader of the clan before she fainted, revived, quieted the others and in a calm voice asked, "What do you think happened, Doctor?" As I explained, they were sad but composed. Sometimes the best thing to do is nothing.

When I inform family members that a loved one has died, I feel most comfortable avoiding euphemisms such as expired, passed on, or departed. I say they died.

Always ask the family if they have any questions, especially in the case of an unexpected or unattended death. If the patient was unattended, the family usually wants to know how they died. Unless it is obviously false, I try to reassure them that their loved one died quietly and was in no pain.

COMPLETE THE DEATH CERTIFICATE ASAP

Our final obligation in the immediate aftermath of a death is completing the Death Certificate. The family needs this document as soon as possible. Many doctors do not realize that insurance claims or estate settlements cannot even begin without a Death Certificate. I have seen a certificate lie on another physician's desk for weeks before completion. It is going to take just as much time to finish this chore a month from now as it will to do it now. Never get involved in childish arguments over who should fill it out. The general public cares nothing about the pecking order among physicians. If it was your patient, fill it out even if your partner was on call and pronounced them dead. If there were multiple physicians and the certificate is on your desk, complete it.

For a bereaved person, getting a legal document declaring their loved one dead can be a devastating, but necessary, event. They don't understand why it should be so difficult to get a physician to do what, by law, cannot be done by anyone else. You can divert much hostility that will be directed at the medical profession in general and at you in particular by doing it promptly.

CARE DOES NOT END WITH THE DEATH CERTIFICATE

Much of what we can do for families after a death depends upon our past relationship with them. If the deceased had been my patient for some time I try to attend the visitation if at all possible. I can usually stop at the church or funeral home on the way home from the office. Other visitors are not reluctant to let you go to the head of the line if you explain that you are the deceased's physician and need to speak to the family. Such a visit takes less than thirty minutes and is long remembered by the family.

I try to send a personal note - not a stock sympathy card - to the family four to six weeks after their loved one dies. I keep it short I just state again that I am sorry, and, if I can, include a personal anecdote about some humorous incident that I recall or something I admired about the deceased. I encourage family members to see me if they have questions or are having problems dealing with the death. If you choose to write, always refer to the deceased by name, never as "your husband" or "your child."

Families have told me that notes from physicians, nurses, and office staff held special meaning. These notes confirm that their loved one really mattered. Almost to a person they also say that they never discard them.

The timing is important. About a month after the death, most of their friends and acquaintances have moved on and no one ever mentions their loved one. A note at this time will do more than Prozac.

KNOW ABOUT THE GRIEF PROCESS

Family members will often come to you for help in dealing with their grief. It behooves you to at least learn the basics about the grief process. Sometimes the most helpful thing you can do is to reassure them that their runaway emotions are normal and that they are not "going crazy." But for you to be able to reassure them, you must know yourself what normal is. There are numerous books dealing with grief and loss. The Compassionate Friends web site listed at the end of chapter eight is a good resource guide for further information.

I have been facilitating a support group for bereaved parents for fifteen years. The three groups of people with whom they are most disappointed are, in order, psychiatrists and counselors, clergy and physicians. They complained that physicians didn't understand, would not spend any time with them and, instead of listening, prescribed a pill and left them feeling abandoned.

If you choose to deal with grieving patients, it will take time. A common problem is that they feel pressured by friends, family, employers, and their physician to hurry up and get well. Contrary to popular belief, they are not "over it" in the allotted one-year. They never get over it. They adapt. They don't "get back to normal." They establish a new normal. The average time it takes a person to adapt to the death of an aged parent is 12-18 months, to the death of a spouse, 2-3 years, and to the death of a child, 4-6 years. These are averages. The time is significantly extended if the death was sudden, unexpected or violent. Healing varies from person to person. Keep in mind that it takes as long as it takes which is much longer than most of us think.

LISTENING IS OFTEN THE BEST THERAPY

What can you do to help someone through the grief process? The most important thing you can do is to listen. There is nothing you can say to fix their problem. They need to talk - a lot. If they cry, even uncontrollably, give them a tissue and wait.

Don't be intimidated by violent emotions. Anger is a natural part of the grieving process. Often anger is directed at a particular doctor, or you. Don't get defensive. Just let them talk. Many times they will level extreme anger towards God. Don't feel compelled to defend Him. God is big enough to take care of Himself. Now is not the time for a theological discussion. Just nod and listen without comment.

GRIEF IS NOT USUALLY CLINICAL DEPRESSION

The fact that they are sad and cry all the time does not necessarily indicate a clinical depression. You're supposed to be sad and cry when your spouse or your child dies. A majority of people does quite well with no medication. They often resent it when the doctor rushes to grab the prescription pad. Unless there is a previous personal history or a strong family history of clinical depression, I wait 2-3 months before trying an antidepressant. An antidepressant corrects a chemical abnormality. If you give a trial of an antidepressant and it is needed, there should be a noticeable improvement. But they will still be sad and grieving at the same level as those who have no clinical depression. I almost never use benzodiazipines, given their propensity for habituation and intensifying true depression.

Frequently grieving people will say that they no longer care to go on living. Many bereaved parents will express such feelings. Explore their feelings but recognize that they almost never have real suicidal ideation or intent.

BE FAMILIAR WITH OTHER SOURCES OF HELP

While nonjudgmental listening is the best thing we have to offer grieving patients, there are a few things that we can do that often prove to be helpful.

Be familiar with local support resources. Many churches have grief support groups. These are most often directed toward people who have experienced the loss of a parent, spouse, adult relative or a friend and can be invaluable for these people. They are usually not helpful for bereaved parents whose loss is so different. Two excellent support groups for bereaved parents are listed in chapter eight.

Unless the grief reaction is unduly prolonged - two to four months - be careful about recommending psychologists or psychiatrists, especially in the case of bereaved parents. Often these professionals' experience in dealing with parents whose children have died is no better than that of ordinary physicians. The majority of parents with whom I have dealt expressed dissatisfaction or outright anger after seeking their services.

Grief counselors can be invaluable if they are good. It is our responsibility to know which ones have proven helpful. Patients are quick to inform us about those who are not. Except in the case of a truly suicidal patient, I feel that a well-informed personal physician who is willing to invest the time can do as much as a psychiatrist.

LITERATURE CAN BE HELPFUL

About a month after my son died, his allergist stopped by my office. He said he didn't know what to say, but he had several books that I might find useful. He was right. I talked with him later, and he said that he had made a ministry of providing books for his patients and acquaintances who had experienced the death of a loved one. Be aware of several books that you can recommend to your patients.

WRITING CAN HELP

Here is one final suggestion that I have found to be

healing for many patients. Encourage them to write ---to keep a journal. They can write on their own schedule and it gives them an outlet for pent-up emotions. It can also serve as a benchmark for their progress. Emotions and perceptions tend to blur during the grief process. On a "down" day they may feel that they are no better off than a year before. Many have told me that looking back at what they had written several months before impressed upon them the real progress that they had made.

WHAT NOT TO SAY

The ancient adage, primum non nocere (first, do no harm), is especially true in what we say. We want to help, but using clichés we have always heard at funerals can prove to be a minefield. We say them with the best of intentions. They may be true, but more often than not they do more harm than good. Remember, the best thing to say is, AI am so sorry." What follows is a list of many of the things bereaved patients have told me that they found hurtful. The list is incomplete, but you will get the idea. A few are particularly painful for bereaved parents. I will discuss these in the section on the death of a child.

You should be over this by now. They will get better when they get better, and our hurrying them doesn't help.

Life goes on. What is this supposed to mean? One of the things that the bereaved sometimes find most infuriating is that life does go on as if nothing has happened.

This too will pass. Probably it will, but for a long time it doesn't feel like it.

Should. One bereaved parent told me that "People just 'should' all over me." Everyone knows what a bereaved person should do. They should go back to work. They should take some time off. They should see a psychiatrist. They shouldn't see a psychiatrist. They should get out more, and on and on. I try to avoid "should" altogether and couch any directive advice in terms such as "You might find it helpful if you'." The one bit of direct advice that I give bereaved families is not to make any irreversible decisions for one year. There is no rush to get rid of the deceased person's clothing or possessions. Their job may seem unbearable, but if they quit and get another, it is likely to be just as unbearable.

At least. Yes, at least the loved one may not be in pain any more, but this is for the family to decide and say.

When we say "At least," it often comes across to the bereaved as minimizing the loss.

It was God's will. It's probably best to avoid religious comments. You will be hard pressed to convince a grief-stricken widow that God willed the drunk driver to run over her spouse or that God willed the heart attack that took the father of her young children. If the bereaved says, "It was God's will," nod but do not elaborate.

Don't try to top the loss. The fact that you had another patient whose wife and two children were killed in an automobile accident will prove scant comfort to a man who has just lost his wife.

Many patients will ask you "Why?" over and over again. "Why" is a metaphysical question for which you have no answer. It's best to say, "I don't know."

CHAPTER EIGHT

WHEN A CHILD DIES

Helping parents cope with the death of a child is one of the hardest things a doctor is called upon to do. This devastating calamity is complicated by the fact that many times the death is sudden and totally unexpected. Children are supposed to bury their parents, not vice versa. Everything mentioned in chapter seven applies even more so in the case of the death of a child. Most people, physicians included, find dealing with bereaved parents particularly difficult because it hits so close to home. We do not even want to imagine ourselves in their place.

HELP PARENTS REMEMBER

In addition to what I have already mentioned, I suggest one other thing that bereaved parents have found useful and for which they have thanked me. I have spoken widely in our area about coping with the loss of a child. As a consequence, I often will get a call from the local emergency room informing me that a child has been killed in an accident and asking if I could come and help. Unless I know the family, I decline. The last thing they need is for a total stranger to show up to fix things while they are in shock. I do ask to speak with the friend or family member who seems to have taken charge. I suggest that at the visitation and/or funeral they have the minister ask friends to write their favorite memory of the deceased child and send it to the family. When I see the family I encourage them to ask their child's friends and teachers to write a remembrance for them. Nowadays, many funeral homes will help the family set up a memorial page on the Internet. Parent after parent has told me that reading these memories was the thing that helped them most. They never discard these stories and they read them again and again. These communications also provide a means for long-term contact with their child's friends.

Most bereaved parents have a deep dread that in time everyone will forget their child. These notes remind them that such is not the case. They will never discard them.

In the case of the death of a child, a personal note from the physician is treasured. I also jot the child's birthday and the day they died in the chart. When I see a parent around one of these significant dates, I try to mention their child by name at the end of the visit. They may shed a tear or two, but they always say, "Thank you."

REASSURE THE PARENTS IF YOU CAN

One of bereaved parents' greatest fears is that their child was in pain or was frightened at the time of death. Physicians are considered experts who can make some accurate determination if their child suffered or was frightened. The majority of children die in accidents, usually involving automobiles. Unless there is irrefutable evidence to the contrary, I assure the parents that their child's injuries were such that they died instantly.

In situations where instant death cannot be proven but where the child was not actually observed to be frightened or in pain, I have found two examples that give parents significant peace of mind.

We have all had patients who, though grievously injured, appeared to be in little pain. Such analgesia was common with many injuries I saw in Vietnam. I briefly explain the role of cerebral endorphins in pain relief and suggest that they were active in their child.

In regard to being frightened I use the example of near death experiences. There are numerous reports of these occurring even in children. As with adults, the hallmark of these experiences is a pervasive sense of peace and tranquility. I suggest that, rather than being frightened, their child was at peace.

Can I prove that such was the case? No. Can anyone prove that it was not? Again, no. But, almost to a person, parents choose to believe that this was the circumstance with their child and are comforted by the thought. I know I was.

It is also helpful to reassure parents that their marriage is not doomed because their child has died. There is a widespread, popular belief that 80% of marriages end in divorce after the death of a child. This urban myth is based on an early study of less than twenty families. In 2006 a well controlled poll of over 25,000 bereaved parents found that the divorce rate after the death of a child is actually less than that of the general population.

SUPPORT GROUPS CAN BE INVALUABLE

Bereaved parents need to talk far more than we have time to listen. They need to tell their stories over and over. Friends, co-workers, and many family members find it almost unbearable to listen. Even well intentioned ones who try, soon drift off after several weeks. There are two national organizations that provide help and an opportunity for parents, grandparents, and siblings to share. They are The Compassionate Friends and Bereaved Parents USA. These organizations combined have over 700 support groups nationwide. Contact information is at the end of this chapter.

WHAT NOT TO SAY AFTER THE DEATH OF A CHILD

Bereaved parents are very sensitive. Take great care in what you say. The clichés mentioned earlier apply to bereaved parents as well. There are a few others that I hear complaints about time and again.

A mother in our support group was irate when her physician said that her child "was better off now." Despite the fact that her child had been severely brain-damaged at birth, was bed-fast and had required care 24 hours a day for 27 years, she was infuriated that someone would suggest that her child was better off dead than with her continued love and care. There are no positives in the death of a child. Don't try to find any.

There are several frequently used clichés unique to bereaved parents.

You're so lucky to have other children. If you say this, get ready to duck. Many a bereaved parent has responded with, "Which of your children could you have die and feel lucky?"

Almost all parents fear that they and others will forget their child. Terms such as closure, getting over it, moving on, and turning loose all imply forgetting, and should be avoided at all times.

I know just how you feel. Unless you have lost a child, you don't.

PARENTS GRIEVE EVEN IF THEIR CHILD NEVER LIVED

There is one final situation that is often mishandled. What should we do in the case of a miscarriage or stillbirth? These parents are often referred to as the forgotten mourners. To the parents, especially to the mother, miscarriage, stillbirth and perinatal death are as devastating as the loss of an older child. For most parents, from the moment the pregnancy test is positive they begin planning for the future. By the second trimester they are convinced that their child will be bright, beautiful and perfect in all ways. When the child dies, they seldom get a sympathy card. In contrast with other bereaved parents they are left with shattered dreams but few, if any, memories to worry about forgetting.

Some of the cruelest "comforting phrases" are used here.

It's not as if it was alive. No comment is needed.

You can always have other children. So what? It was this child they had hopes and dreams for.

Finally, physicians need to realize that explanations about a "blighted ovum" usually are not helpful.

The same things mentioned above apply to the parents of a miscarried or stillborn child. They are always grateful for a follow-up note or call. If the child was named, refer to it by its name.

If the parents want to hold the baby before release to the funeral home, let them - for as long as they wish.

They cannot go home with a baby as they dreamed, but don't send them home empty-handed. If there are ultrasounds of the baby, give them a copy. Take pictures of the baby. Parents may not want them at that moment, but they will often return to retrieve them later. Give them a copy of the ID footprints, the stocking cap, the gown, a teddy bear or whatever parents are customarily given at your hospital. Anything that points to the reality and existence of their child is almost always accepted and treasured.

The death of a child is the most devastating loss any parent will ever face. If we can help - even a little - we will have done something of lasting value.

One of the most treasured compliments I ever received as a physician was from a patient I cared for after her son drowned. When I left practice twenty years later she wrote me a note and said, "In the absolutely worst time of my life, you were there, and you cared. Thank you."

SUPPORT GROUPS

THE COMPASSIONATE FRIENDS

www.compassionatefriends.org

PH-630-990-0010

169

Toll Free-877-969-0010

FAX-630-990-0246

BEREAVED PARENTS, USA

www.bereavedparentsusa.org

CHAPTER NINE
TAKING CARE OF YOURSELF

It is well to superintend the sick and make them well, to care for the healthy and keep them well, and also to care for oneself.

-Hippocrates

Hippocrates was right. Many, perhaps most, physicians are too rushed and too busy to enjoy fully their medical practices or their lives. The damage perpetual hurry causes us and our family is, in large part, self-inflicted.

I think there are two major sources of our problems. The first is real, or perceived, financial needs. The second is psychological.

WE CAN'T AFFORD TO TAKE CARE OF OURSELVES

A large number, perhaps a majority, of young physicians cannot slow down enough to enjoy themselves and their families due to the need to generate maximal income.

Many well-intentioned physicians stumble unaware into the quicksand of financial obligation where the need to earn as much as possible overwhelms whatever altruistic goals they had when they first entered medicine. There are three common situations that suck us in. All three are to a large degree preventable.

I'M SO FAR IN DEBT I'LL NEVER CATCH UP

The most common reason for slipping into the maximal income mode is the need to pay off large loans for medical education. As with credit card and other debts, this is better prevented than remedied. Time and again I have interviewed young physicians seeking practice opportunities who have just completed their residencies. They have purchased a house, two cars, usually expensive, and have one or two children - all financed by loans. Banks are more than willing to lend you money, but the time comes when you must pay it back. Therein lies the problem. Debt limits your practice possibilities. There is a growing shortage of family practitioners and pediatricians, which I think is in large part due to the need to pay off huge loans used to finance medical education. Since these specialties are at the bottom of the physician income pyramid, many who might otherwise become primary care physicians must opt for more highly compensated specialties.

Even worse, the effort to repay requires so much time and work that all too often these physicians must compromise their practice principles or their family - often both.

When I was in medical training, loans were not as forthcoming. My family was unable to give me any assistance at all for college or medical school. Yet, I left my training debt free. Most of my classmates and fellow house staff also entered practice relatively free of debt. We had one cheap car, lived in inexpensive rental housing, worked part-time ("moonlighted"), postponed children and some joined the military. The military option for financing medical school and training still exists. Although you must pay back in time rather than money, you can gain valuable experience and enter private practice with minimal debt and in control of your own fate. Quite often I hear in the doctors' lounge, "There's no free lunch." This is usually said in reference to patients who are poor, unemployed or uninsured. In a sense they are right. There is no free lunch - even for physicians.

YOU MUST KNOW BUSINESS AS WELL AS MEDICINE

Many doctors wind up on a spirit-sapping financial treadmill due to economic naivete. They just do not have a clue about finances or running a business. As a result they must scramble for maximal income to offset managerial ineptitude. When we exit training, most of us are ill-prepared to manage payrolls, rent, and the other business necessities of a medical practice. Gone are the days when you could make up for poor management of your practice by raising your fees. If you possess few business skills it might be best to have a business manager from the outset, but be sure you control the manager, not vice versa. The same holds true if you enter an established group practice or are employed by a hospital or managed care organization. In each of these cases, it is your responsibility to maintain a practice focused on the patients' physical and emotional needs rather than on your or your employer's financial desires.

HOW MUCH DO YOU REALLY NEED?

The final reason for slipping into the quagmire of debt is that, after so many years of financial deprivation, many young physicians establish a lifestyle that requires maximal income to maintain. They have an unrealistic idea of what a physician's life style should be. They often pattern themselves after someone who has been in a successful practice for years, and they attempt to adopt a similar way of living immediately. Just as living beyond your means on loans during training can warp the type of medicine you must practice, so can adopting the life style of the rich and famous.

It is not even necessary. How many physicians have you met who were really financially deprived? Besides that, the true joy in medicine does not come from what we get but from what we give. The best defense against developing an unaffordable life style is to decide, (with your spouse if you're married), long before you finish your training, what income you think is necessary to educate the children, fund retirement and have a reasonable standard of living. Then work hard enough to attain that. When you reach your goal, take on a partner - in essence, buy back your time. If you prefer to work alone, limit your practice. Go beyond that and you will find that you must sacrifice your patients, your family, and yourself for what will most likely have the taste of ashes.

MANY OF US HAVE A COMMON MALADY A PERSONAL STORY

There are some psychological reasons that many physicians have problems. I believe that the very qualities that enable many of us to get through medical school and residencies predispose us to living less than full lives. What follows is a description of me, but I am convinced that it is accurate for many of my classmates, colleagues, and significant numbers of current medical students and residents. Perhaps the situation will change with the increasing number of females entering medicine, but that remains to be seen.

For the most part we are Type A plus personalities. We are always pressed for time. We are focused and single-minded. We need to be in control. Most of us are, to a large degree, perfectionists who suffer fools lightly. (A fool being anyone who inconveniences us.) We tend to be driven and hard-working. Witness the barely suppressed pride with which we relate how many hours we worked last week or that we got only five hours sleep on our last weekend on call.

Our personality type leads to much of the inappropriate behavior I have mentioned previously. Many of us want to change but just do not seem able to. It is possible, but some of us have to learn the hard way.

I have always had a wonderful relationship with my patients. The other doctors at our hospital respected me. Beyond that, however, the previous description was me - in spades. The nurses respected me as a clinician but disliked me as a person and avoided me as much as possible. I had a short fuse. I was overbearing and sarcastic.

In the chapter on dealing with nurses I did most of what I cautioned should not be done. In brief, I was a jerk. My patients and my practice many times came before my family. I knew how I was behaving and hated it, but I could never improve. I was not alone. Others on our staff behaved as I did. We want to change but cannot.

The question is, Why? Much of it goes back to our Type A, perfectionist personalities. But there is more to it than that. Many of us cannot differentiate big problems from small ones. Everything is an emergency. We get the same rush of adrenaline and catecholamines from a missed lab test, an inappropriate phone call, or a perceived dump from the ER as we do from a cardiac arrest. We respond to each with equal aggression.

This was me. As a result, I was respected but not well-liked.

When I left active hospital practice, I was one of the best-liked physicians on our staff. I have not said an unkind word to a nurse since June 6, 1992.

How can I be so sure of the date? I was on call that weekend. At 4 a.m. I received a phone call informing me that my 21 year-old son had been murdered in another state. I didn't analyze it until later, but in less than five minutes I learned what was important and what was not. My behavior changed almost at once. I have seen similar transformations in others after heart attacks, close calls with cancer, or near fatal accidents.

Take time to look at your classmates, fellow residents, other physicians and yourself. Many behave much as I did. Most will be as dissatisfied as I was. I hope they can change course less painfully than I did.

Can we learn to live life more fully? Can we learn empathy and caring? It's hard, but I believe it's possible. The following has been a tremendous help to me. You might find it useful.

WE NEED TO SEE LIFE DIFFERENTLY

For many of us, happiness is always "out there." When I get the college grind over with, I'll be in medical school and on my way. When I get into my residency, I'll be out from under all the tests and scut work that get dumped on me and be a real doctor. That will be great. When I finish my residency, I'll be in private practice and my own boss - no more playing second fiddle. When I get all my student loans paid off, I can relax and enjoy the fruits of my labor. When this, when that, but never now.

We continue to rush headlong through life, forgetting the quaint, but true, old saying, "Happiness is a journey, not a destination." We seldom slow down and notice what is going on around us. Without thinking, we act and react in familiar, repeated patterns. We live our lives on automatic pilot.

How can we slow down and really savor the joys that medicine and life offer?

An oncologist friend of mine taught me an exercise that has proven life changing for both of us. Each evening I take a few minutes to jot in a journal the answers to four questions:

What new or interesting thing did I learn about someone today?

What inspired me today?

What moved, or touched me today?

What did I do that made a difference to anyone today?

The answers are not long essays on life - just brief

observations. I don't consciously edit the entries. They are for me, not others. But they make me stop and notice strangers, my patients, my coworkers, my friends, my family, and me. At first these were all retrospective. Later, I became aware of events as they occurred. I began to see the world differently. Inspiring, meaningful things happened every day. I just had not noticed them before.

As I became aware of this new spectrum of life, my attitude changed. Others seemed to notice. Nurses no longer walked on eggshells. My family was more at ease. My patients opened their lives to me.

Some say empathy cannot be taught. To some degree it cannot. But recording the answers to these questions daily have made me more insightful into the human condition and yes, more empathetic.

Try it. You, too, might learn to see life differently.

Nothing will sustain you more potently than the power to recognize in your humdrum routine, as perhaps it may be thought, the true poetry of life: the poetry of the commonplace, of the ordinary man, of the plain, toil-worn woman, with their loves, their joys, their sorrows, and their griefs.

- Sir William Osler

Made in the USA
Coppell, TX
06 January 2023

10553717R00101